"Birkel is a true trailblazer who has created a solid, cutting edge program for recovery and reemployment." —LEONARD FLORENCE

"Professionals In Transition gave me the emotional support and understanding when I was at the lowest point in my life. People need you and PIT more than ever." —TAD TADLOCK

"…I was able to stretch my career thinking and get on the right track as to where I wanted my job to take me." —CHANDLER LAMB

"*Career Bounce-Back!* taught me how to network—not just that I needed to network. The methods really work. It is the best networking book—period." —CHUCK ROHDA

"…I learned more today than I have in the three months that I have been out of work." —ANDY DORER

"Thank you for 'hearing the need' through your own experiences and courageously stepping up to the plate to begin Professionals In Transition." —LINDA L. ALLGOOD

"*Career Bounce-Back!*…has helped thousands endure the temporary situation called job loss. As a retired career senior officer with the United States military, I found Damian's book invaluable helping me make the difficult transition into the corporate business community. His foresight calmed my fears, focused my energy and saved me countless wasted hours during my job search. Thanks Damian for bringing light into the darkness of transition." —L. STEPHEN ROBINSON

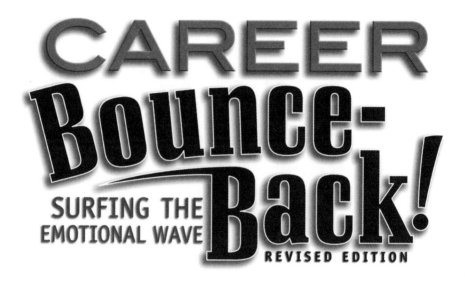

CAREER
Bounce-Back!
SURFING THE
EMOTIONAL WAVE
Back!
REVISED EDITION

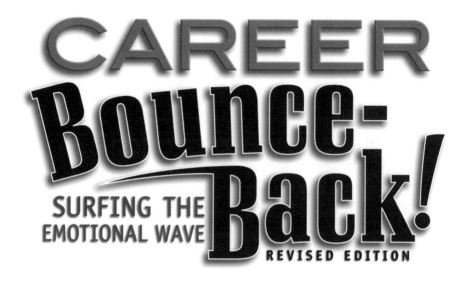

CAREER Bounce-Back!

SURFING THE EMOTIONAL WAVE

REVISED EDITION

J. Damian Birkel
with Stacey J. Miller

The Professionals In Transition®
Guide to Recovery & Reemployment

PO Box 11252, Winston-Salem, NC 27116-1252

Applied for Library of Congress Cataloging-in-Publication Data.
ISBN 0-9720629-0-4

Design and layout by Whitline Ink Incorporated *e-mail*—bookdesign@yadtel.net
E-wave graphic copyright ©2002 Cheryl Powell
Printed in the United States of America

05 04 03 02   5 4 3 2 1

I lost my job twice in a ten-year period. Each time I searched for a road map to reemployment, and promised never to forget what it was like to be unemployed. Professionals In Transition and the Career Bounce-Back! *book, the accompanying workbook, and networking video is that promise kept. Thank you for giving me the opportunity to share these tips, tools, and techniques that we have learned from the trenches of reemployment. At Professionals In Transition we always say that "unemployment is a temporary condition!"*

Career Bounce-Back! *is dedicated to your reemployment journey.*

All the Best,

—J. Damian Birkel

contents

Acknowledgments...xv
Foreword xvii
Introduction:
From Pink Slips to Paychecks:
Paving the Way for Job Seekers and Job Changers 1
   History of Professionals In Transition 3
Organization 9

CHAPTER 1

A Bridge Is a Terrible Thing to Burn:
Parting Company Productively with Your Employer and Colleagues....11

   Pink Slips for All...12
   The Day of Reckoning 12
   Negotiating Again...13
     When and How You Leave 15
     Severance Package...15
     Health Insurance...16
   Getting Legal Help 18
   Spinning Your Story 19
   Taking Care of Business 20
   Taking It with You 20
   Saying a Proper Farewell 22
   Relationships After Termination 23
   Gathering References 24
   Unemployment Compensation 25
   Action Plan Recap...26

CHAPTER 2

The Stark Truth About Job Loss:
Understanding the Process of Transition 29

   Life After Unemployment 30
   The Emotional Wave of Unemployment 30
   Stage 1: Shock and Denial 33
     Coping With Shock and Denial 34
   Stage 2: Fear and Panic...34
     Coping with Fear and Panic....................................36

Stage 3: Anger 36
  Coping with Anger 38
Stage 4: Bargaining 39
  Coping with Bargaining 40
Stage 5: Depression 41
  Coping with Depression 42
Stage 6: Temporary Acceptance 43
  Coping with Temporary Acceptance 44
Moving On 45

CHAPTER 3

Home and Hearth:
Guiding Your Family Through the Challenges of Unemployment 47

The Worst that Can Happen 47
You're in It Together 48
The Family Wave 49
As the World Turns Downward 50
  Powerlessness..51
  Rising Tensions 52
What Else You Can Do 54
  Communicate 54
  Establish a New Role for Yourself 55
  Maintain Normality..55
Payoffs of Unemployment 57

CHAPTER 4

Begin the Bounce-Back Beguine:
Reinventing the Professional You 59

What Should You Do? 60
  Step 1: Figure Out Where You've Been...........................62
  Step 2: Compare Work Experiences 63
  Step 3: Do a Quick Take...63
  Step 4: Find the Professional You 64
  Step 5: Dream A Dream...65
Where Should You Do It?..67
  Step 6: Survey the Field 67
  Step 7: Writing Out a Plan...69
Exploring Alternatives 70
  Step 8: Create a Mission Statement and Career Summary 72
Putting Your Job Plan into Action 73

Establish a Daily Routine 73
Develop a Winning Attitude 73
Create an Efficient "Office" Space 74
Track Results 75

CHAPTER 5

How to Find Good Help Nowadays:

Using Low-Cost/No-Cost Job-Hunting Resources 77
  Rebuilding Your Network...78
  Recruitment Firms 79
    Choosing a Recruiter 79
    Of Cold Calls and Cold Shoulders 80
    The Networking Solution 81
    Do Your Homework 82
  Career Counseling 84
    Finding the Right Career Counseling....................................84
    Low-Cost or No-Cost Alternatives 85
  Job Hunting High-Tech Style..86
    Track Your Online Hours 87
    Electronic Networking 88
    Other Electronic Tools 90

CHAPTER 6

Campaign for Success:

Using Résumés and Cover Letters to Market Yourself Effectively 91
  Making Every Second Count 91
    Putting Résumés and Cover Letters into Perspective 92
    What Use Are They?..93
    Résumés and Cover Letters that Survive the Cut.................94
    Multiple Written Pitches 95
    Guidelines for Crafting Résumés 96
    Guidelines for Crafting Cover Letters....................................98
    Electronic Résumés and Cover Letters 99
    Help with Your Résumé and Cover Letter 102

CHAPTER 7

The Shortest Path to Reemployment:

Building a Network of Allies 105
  Speeding Up Your Job Search...105
  The Golden Rules of Networking 107

Prerequisite: Do Your Homework 108
How to Begin Informational Interviews 109
  Why You Need Referrals 110
  How to Begin 110
  At the Top 111
  Landing an Informational Interview 111
  Surviving the Telephone Screening Process 112
  Other Timing Tips 112
  When They Don't Respond 113
  Setting Up a Meeting 114
  At the Meeting 115
  Saying Goodbye 116
  Following Through 117
  After the Interview 117
Random but Wonderful 118

<hr>

CHAPTER 8

Cheek-to-Cheek, Pen-to-Paper:
Finessing Every Interview and Negotiation 119
  The Final Frontier 119
  The Right Mindset 120
  Transferable Interviewing Skills 121
  Solving the Problem 122
  Project a Winning Attitude 123
  Your Needs 125
  Your Expectations 126
  Second Interview and Beyond 127
  Moving on After Rejection..128
  The Job Offer 129
  Negotiation 130
  Evaluating the Job 131

Appendix A:
  PIT's Top Ten Guerrilla Job-Hunting Tactics:
  Cutting Edge Strategies from Members of PIT Support Groups 133
Appendix B:
  The Essential Eclectic Library:
  Helpful Books, Magazines, and Other Resources 137
Author's Note 145
Index 147

thank you

A portion of the proceeds from your purchase of *Career Bounce-Back!* will be contributed to the Professionals In Transition® Paying-It-Forward™ Fund of the Winston-Salem Foundation.

Professionals In Transition Support Group, Inc. (PIT®) is a volunteer-driven, nonprofit organization that helps people find jobs. The organization is one of the oldest tax-exempt, 501(c)(3) service organizations in the United States, offering weekly networking and job search support group meetings. PIT does not receive local, state, or federal funding, nor is it a United Way agency. PIT is dependent on friends, alumni, the faith community, and foundation grants for operating support.

The Paying-It-Forward Fund "is designed to provide operating revenue for Professionals In Transition. Income from the fund will enable the organization to fulfill its mission of reaching out to the unemployed and the underemployed and helping deal with the experiences of reemployment in an atmosphere of confidentiality, integrity, and trust," at no cost to participants.

If you would like to make a tax-deductible contribution to Professionals In Transition, please send your donation to:

The Professionals In Transition Paying-It-Forward Fund
The Winston-Salem Foundation
860 West Fifth Street
Winston-Salem, NC 27101-2506
(336) 725-2382

Thank you for helping Professionals In Transition!

acknowledgments

*C*areer Bounce-Back! would have never been written without my coauthor, Stacey J. Miller. Her knowledge, enthusiasm, persistence, and hard work are evident on every page. Charles D. Nanney, John Jackman, Melvin Scales, John Colthar, Chuck Chambers, and Donna Birkel are the catalysts behind this newly-revised edition. They took a considerable risk, and I acknowledge their vision, commitment, and enthusiasm. Thank you for making this revised edition and workbook and accompanying videotape series happen.

Special thanks to Barry Boyd, John Eiffe, Roger Pike, Carolyn and Jerry Sink, for many years of extraordinary service. I'm also grateful for the numerous contributions of time, talent, and treasure made by our PIT board members since 1992. Thanks also to Chris McGee and Pat McPhail, who were there at the beginning of PIT.

Thanks also to Ron Jones, Kathleen Natalie, Roger Pike, and John Colthar for their numerous contributions at our PIT chapters. I am deeply grateful to Marcia Cole, executive director of the American Red Cross, Winston-Salem chapter (home of PIT meetings since 1992); to Dr. Richard Randolph, senior pastor of Christ United Methodist Church (original home for our Greensboro Chapter); and to Barbara Esquibel, president; and Leigh Anne Good, chairman of the Greensboro Jaycees (host and PIT chapter partner in Greensboro).

To our many volunteer PIT meeting facilitators, I thank you for your enthusiasm, energy, commitment, and countless hours of dedication. To the over one thousand PIT members, and the over half a million people whose lives we have had the privilege to touch through www.jobsearching.org, I offer my gratitude.

Without the support of Chuck Chambers, I would have never had the courage to start Professionals In Transition. Chuck's guiding principles and philosophy of "service first" empowered me to start PIT and also write the first edition when we were at Sara Lee Direct. He was also instrumental in helping PIT receive start-up funding from our initial foundation partners, The Winston-Salem Foundation, and the Community Foundation of Greater Greensboro. Chuck also introduced me to the power of audio learning where I have acquired knowledge from many experts including: Earl Nightengale, Norman Vincent Peale, Stephen Covey, Dale Carnegie, and Zig Ziglar.

Al Renna, president and CEO of Family Services, Inc., has served as my nonprofit mentor since 1997, helping me transition from a corporate product-marketing manager to a nonprofit executive. Al's insight, knowledge, patience, humor, and many long nights of tutoring me are deeply appreciated.

Nido Qubein is the chairman of Creative Services, Inc., an international management and consulting firm. He is also chairman of McNeill Lehman, Inc., Business Life, Inc., and Great Harvest Bread Company with 200 stores in 35 states. Toastmasters International named him top business and commerce speaker and awarded him the Golden Gavel Medal. Nido taught me the fine art of effective communication. He is both a friend and mentor. Thank you, Nido, for changing my life!

My gratitude to author and TV personality Tom O'Neal; Alex Saenz; Dr. John P. Wilson, Ph.D.; Dr. Elisabeth Kubler-Ross, author of *On Death On Dying*; and Richard Nelson Bolles, author of *What Color Is Your Parachute?*, who believed in this project from its inception. My appreciation goes to Tom Jennings, Hector McEachern, Randall Henion, Dick and Gay Wilson, and Sara Lee Direct friends including Steve Nachman, Steve Guttenberg, Jackie and Tim Dickson, Angela and Rodney Mullins, Karen Isgett, and Chuck Whitley.

Special thanks to Cheryl Powell, Scott Whitaker, and Emily Sarah Lineback for their creative input and many hours of help in creating the new edition of *Career Bounce-Back!,* and to Steven Bennett for his help developing the original manuscript and to Barbara Thornton, for her feedback on Chapter 1.

Finally, *Career Bounce-Back!* would not have been possible without the grace of God and the love and support of my family. To my loving wife, Donna, for more than 25 years of marriage, patience, unwavering support, and belief in me: I thank you daily, as the earth thanks the sun. And to my wonderful children, Annie and John, thank you for your unconditional love.

foreword

*C*areer Bounce-Back! offers a solid, cutting-edge program for recovery and reemployment with proven strategies which include:

- ■ Coping with the terror and trauma of downsizing.
- ■ Managing the emotional wave of unemployment.
- ■ Developing strategies to protect yourself and your family.
- ■ Finding the hidden job market through the power of informational interviewing.

I am delighted that Damian has asked me to write the foreword to the new edition of *Career Bounce-Back!* Damian has, for the first time, mapped out the psychological stages of job loss and provides tips, tools, and techniques for coming to terms with job loss and reentering the workforce. I congratulate Damian for his unique and important contribution to the literature on careers and for his trailblazing efforts to create Professionals In Transition Support Group, Inc. PIT has received national and international recognition as one of the oldest nonprofit job-searching support groups in North America.

You can help yourself and Professionals In Transition Support Groups by reading and learning from this book. A portion of the proceeds from every purchase is being donated to the Professionals In Transition Paying-It-Forward Fund of the Winston-Salem Foundation. This fund enables PIT to continue to help people find jobs by offering emotional support, networking, and job-searching tools in an atmosphere of confidentiality, integrity, and trust.

I encourage anyone who is in transition now, or who may be in the future, to turn to *Career Bounce-Back!* for inspiration and guidance.

—Nido Qubein

Nido Qubein is chairman of an international consulting firm and chairman of McNeill Lehman, Inc., Business Life, Inc., and Great Harvest Bread Company with 200 stores in 35 states, and recipient of the highest award given to professional speakers including the Cavett (known as the Oscar of professional speaking) and the Council of Peers Award of Excellence. He has served as president of the National Speakers Association and holds a Doctor of Law degree from his alma mater, and is recipient of the Ellis Island Congressional Medal of Honor along with dozens of other honors and distinctions. A much-in-demand speaker, Nido has also written many books and recorded scores of audio learning programs. He is a "business insider" with extensive boardroom exposure and is an entrepreneur with active interests in real estate, advertising, and banking.

introduction

From Pink Slips
to Paychecks

*Paving the Way for Job Seekers
and Job Changers*

Two months after receiving a pink slip, Frank, an industrial engineer, trudged down the stairs of the Red Cross building in Winston-Salem, North Carolina. Entering the executive conference room, he quietly made his way to a vacant seat, oblivious to the pleasant chatter around him, and stared at the floor. Frank felt awkward about coming to a support group, but his unemployment benefits were running out, bills were piling up, and after three months of constant rejection, he was tired of struggling to find a job on his own. When he looked up, he was startled to see my outstretched hand.

"Welcome to your first Professionals In Transition meeting," I warmly greeted him. "We're glad you're here and want you to know that from this moment on, you're not alone."

I returned to my seat and called the meeting to order. Frank listened as PIT members shared their job-searching experiences of the prior week, exchanged ideas and insights about reemployment, and offered each other comfort, understanding, support, perspective, and potential job leads.

When it was his turn, Frank shared his feelings of anger and emptiness with the rest of the group. As he spoke, the others nodded. He intuitively understood that many of the people in the room had had similar experiences and would be willing to help him work through his anguish. By the end of the meeting, he felt better than he had for weeks.

A month or so later, Frank was among the first members to arrive at the PIT meeting. He happened to sit next to a recently laid-off engineer, and the two enthusiastically exchanged shop talk until the meeting began. When I opened the floor for the information exchange, Frank announced: "I came across a trade magazine ad that I want to share with the group. A local engineering company is looking for a secretary for the human resources department. If anybody's interested in getting more information, talk to me after the meeting." The following week, Anne, who'd been attending PIT meetings for three months, happily told the group that she'd followed up Frank's lead and was starting her new job the following Monday.

Frank's "graduation" from PIT took place two months later. It was Anne who helped him; she came to a meeting expressly to inform him about an opening at her company, and Frank nailed the job after two interviews. He came to the following meeting with a deli tray, soda, and dessert, and announced: "I got the job!" He told us his reemployment story and recognized Anne for her help in making the job connection that ultimately led to his new position.

Although he gladly puts in fifty hours a week nowadays, he still finds time to attend a PIT meeting each month to let members know about employment leads he stumbles upon. "After all," he smiles, "isn't it my responsibility to give something back to the community that helped me find a light at the end of a very long, dark tunnel?"

History of Professionals in Transition

Since its inception in February 1992, Professionals In Transition Support Group, Inc. has helped hundreds of members like Frank rebuild their self-esteem and restart their careers. A nonprofit and nonsectarian support group, PIT is a forum where people in career transition can share information, generate ideas, create options, and provide perspective—all in an environment of confidentiality, integrity, and trust. Members meet weekly to help one another face the many challenges of unemployment and underemployment and provide each other with support, feedback, and empathy. Ultimately, they look forward to sharing the triumph of reemployment.

As PIT's founder, I originally intended to help professionals who had lost their jobs begin the lengthy, and often painful, climb to reemployment. Much to my amazement and gratification, I found that PIT members didn't need my help; they helped one another. People came to meetings brimming with information that they were willing to exchange with other job seekers. PIT became a magnet for those who would selflessly lend a hand to others—strangers with whom they often had little in common beyond the unemployment experience—just because it was the right thing to do. That positive energy came back to them, time and again, in the form of recovery from job-loss grief, renewed self-esteem, potential job connections, and, ultimately, reemployment.

The idea for an organization like PIT arose from my own intimate encounter with a brutal layoff back in February 1990. I had just relocated from Cleveland, my lifelong residence, with my wife, Donna, and two young children—Annie, seven, and John, three—to accept a more prestigious marketing/merchandising position at a Fortune Fifty corporation in North Carolina. Five weeks after we unpacked the last box in our new home—which we'd bought on the strength of the generous salary I was to earn—my new employer called a companywide meeting amid rampant rumors of a corporate takeover. My coworkers and I wore red in honor of the impending carnage. Before "Bloody Monday" ended, 98 percent of the company's employees had been given their walking papers. We were informed, however, that we could apply for a limited number of positions within the corporation. This understandably turned colleague against colleague, and even supervisor against subordinate. Eventually, all of the support personnel and the majority of upper management were placed within other divisions. Practically all of the middle managers, however, were wiped out and immediately sent to an outplacement firm. One minute I had a career, and the next minute I didn't.

Had I been back in Cleveland, I would have turned to relatives, close friends, countless acquaintances, and my priest for counsel, comfort, and commiseration. As it was, spending too much of my time in those first weeks on business trips meant I really hadn't settled down in my new home. With all the evening and weekend hours I'd put into work even when I wasn't on the road, I hadn't met many people outside of work, nor had I formed any close community ties. Now I had no one other than my family to help me. I was utterly on my own to deal with the shock, grief, guilt, bewilderment, shame, and anger. Overnight, my professional world came crashing down. As I struggled to pick myself up and move on with my life, I mused: *There has to be a better way. Isn't there anyone who can help me?* I searched in vain for an organization that could put me on the road to reemployment. In the past, Al-Anon had gently guided me through the process of dealing with a family member's alcoholism. Surely there was a similar organization for those who were unemployed!

I didn't need someone to hold my hand; rather, I wanted to find people who would understand what I was going through and help me make connections in the community. During that time, the seed of an idea was planted: If there isn't such an organization, why not start one?

Before long, I got a chance to fulfill that dream. My quest for a job, which lasted through many excruciatingly long and painful months, ended successfully in September 1990, when I settled into a new position as a product marketing manager for a different division of the same corporation. About a year later, on November 14, 1991, I went to lunch with a former colleague, Chris McGee. Chris and I had worked together as loaned executives for United Way while we looked for full-time work. I found my current permanent position; he wasn't as lucky and remained in transition.

Now, as we dined on chop suey, we commiserated about how difficult it was to penetrate the professional network of a small town. We agreed that it was demoralizing to sit at home, day after day, waiting for the phone to ring. In a burst of inspiration, I shared with Chris my fantasy about starting a job support group.

His face lit up as I described my idea, and I knew I'd struck a responsive chord. He enthusiastically encouraged me to take my plan to the next level. He introduced me to Pat McPhail, a career counselor who was helping him find a job. A week later, the three of us met to toss around ideas for creating a support group for workers in flux. That conversation helped me define the dream organization's two main goals: to create "safe space" where we could discuss the multiple issues of the reemployment process, and to provide each other with information, job leads, perspective, hope, and to share our job-hunting experiences. But would it work? The only way to find out was to try.

Chris convinced the local Red Cross chapter to donate space for a meeting. We passed out fliers in supermarkets, newsstands, libraries, bookstores, restaurants, churches—anywhere we could find people congregating. I also placed a notice in the calendar sections of the local newspapers, listing my home phone number and encouraging people to call for more information about the upcoming meeting.

Thus was Professionals In Transition born. At the first meeting, the grand total attendance was four, as an unemployed research analyst, John, joined Chris, Pat, and me. We three listened as John poured out his anger and grief, and we responded by telling him about our own struggles with unemployment. This was the first time that any of us had discussed the pain of job loss openly and without fear of judgment; our relief in finding an outlet for our emotions was palpable.

During the next few weeks, we worked together to develop a standard agenda for future meetings. What we came up with was not unlike Al-Anon's; indeed, my experience as an Al-Anon member gave me some good insights into how PIT meetings might be structured.

As more PIT meetings were held, we began to get the hang of it, and gradually some standardization took form.

As members arrived on Thursday evenings, they took seats at tables arranged in a U-shape in the executive conference room of the local Red Cross building. Our meetings were divided into three segments. During part one, the information exchange, we made general announcements, presented job opportunities, and offered updates on PITAs (Professionals In Transition Alumni). More and more, alumni attended the meetings regularly and served as examples of success, standing ready to help newcomers who were in transition.

The first part of the meeting often concluded with a graduation ceremony, during which a PIT member formally announced that he or she had landed a new job and told the group the reemployment story. The member, now a new PITA, usually celebrated by sharing pizza or other light fare with the group. I then had the pleasure of awarding the new alum with a PIT Graduation Certificate.

During part two of the meeting, members introduced themselves and took turns sharing their job-hunting experiences and recounting the emotional weather of the prior week. Finally, during the less-structured "fellowship exchange," which was the third part of the meeting, members and PITAs offered one another job leads, feedback, and advice.

Although the meetings already seemed productive and helpful, I knew that I was largely shooting from the hip. Although I'd studied psychology back in my undergraduate days, I certainly wasn't qualified to be a career counselor. Yet I sensed a fundamental need for the support group to be nonprofessional and volunteer-run, guiding job seekers through the entire reemployment process and covering bases that other job support resources overlooked or omitted. So I embarked on a self-imposed "homework" assignment.

Most of us have dealt with the loss of loved ones, and we have some sense of how to deal with death. We hold a funeral, our relatives come into town, friends cook us meals, and people support us and understand why we're crying. On the other hand, when we lose our jobs, there's no socially acceptable way of working through our grief. My hope was that PIT could provide a structure for people who were coping with job loss. But I had to learn more about the relationship between unemployment and the grieving process before turning PIT into the organization I'd envisioned.

For several months, I read every article about unemployment that I could find. To my surprise, I discovered that few of them, if any, addressed the grief element of job loss. I remained convinced, though, that losing a job was similar in many respects to losing a loved one. So I switched gears and began reading about the grief associated with death and dying. In short order, I filled three binders, each six inches thick, with what I considered critical information about the grieving process and how it related to unemployment.

Next, I distilled the highlights of what I'd learned into a succinct, one-page chart. No, I didn't develop a groundbreaking theory; I simply described and clarified the connection between job loss and the grieving process, a relationship that the experts seemed to have overlooked. I felt that I was on the right track and wanted to talk with others who could verify my findings.

I first turned to my former Cleveland State University professor and long-time friend, John P. Wilson, Ph.D., one of the nation's foremost authorities on post-traumatic stress disorder. John acted as a sounding board and encouraged me to contact one of his former colleagues, Dr. Elisabeth Kübler-Ross, the renowned authority on death and dying.

I wrote a letter to Dr. Kübler-Ross, describing my ideas about the connection between death and dying and job loss. To my delight, she graciously invited me to discuss the details with her in person. During a meeting at her farmhouse in Headwaters, Virginia, she confirmed: "A loss is a loss is a loss. It doesn't make any difference whether it's job loss or a death in the family." Her theories and practices, she said, definitely could be adapted to PIT members and anyone else who had lost his or her livelihood. She and I then spent an entire morning discussing just how this could be done. A consummate teacher, she clearly rejoiced in imparting her knowledge and exchanging ideas with me. We feasted on the freshly picked fruit, homemade sourdough bread, and imported Norwegian strawberry jam that I'd brought (as I couldn't afford to pay her for her time), and I came away with a renewed clarity and commitment to put my plan into action.

The grieving process, as Dr. Kübler-Ross and I redefined it for PIT members, became the core of the "bounce-back" program. As the organization grew, the program evolved naturally. We modified it and added new elements based on feedback from our members and our alumni. The alumni actually began to call themselves PITAs, and they returned to help others work through the bounce-back process. They pitched in to help find work for people like Glen, an unemployed hardware salesman who had recently relocated to North Carolina and didn't know a soul.

At his first PIT meeting, a member mentioned to Glen that a PITA he knew was working for a local home improvement chain. Glen contacted the PITA, who advised him to call the store's recruiter and "let him know you're a PIT member to cut through the red tape." One phone call was all it took; Glen scored an interview the following week, and within a month, he had a job. Within a year, he worked his way up to store manager.

With a steady flow of alumni, PIT grew into something far bigger and more powerful than I had ever dreamed. PIT members and alumni contributed ideas and insights and turned the organization into a soup-to-nuts bounce-back program revolving around the concepts of "heal your soul first, then seek a job" and "help others as you would like to be helped." You'll be helped by applying the battle-tested strategies of over one thousand members to your own situation. This book provides the blueprint you need for success.

It is my ultimate goal to turn Professionals In Transition into a national support network. You can monitor our progress at our non-profit Web site at www.jobsearching.org. In addition, you can learn more about Professsionals In Transition and post your résumé. If you would like to order an accompanying workbook or videotape, please visit www.careerbounceback.com. As always, a portion of the proceeds will be donated to the The Professionals In Transition Pay-ing-It-Forward Fund.

Organization

In this book, I share the complete Career Bounce-Back! Program™ from the beginning. As Chapter 1 explains, it is possible to part company with employers productively and with some measure of dignity, security, and well-being. In that chapter, I also offer a checklist of the most critical issues you must address, and advice for handling some of the most difficult and awkward tasks.

Chapter 2 shows you how to identify and manage the stages of job-loss grief before negative feelings sabotage your career. You'll also discover the common physical stress symptoms that you're likely to experience during the "mourning" process.

Chapter 3 guides you through the process of extending your healing process to help family members bounce back from grief. I also show you the hidden, long-term payoffs that unemployment can have for you as well as for your spouse, children, and other relatives.

At this point, you are probably ready to move on, and the materials I present in Chapter 4 help you identify your changing skills, needs, and goals; they then show you how to translate that knowledge into a career plan.

You may be seeking help with your job search. I reveal the pros and cons associated with executive placement firms, job placement firms, and career counselors in Chapter 5. In addition, I share innovative techniques for using the latest electronic job-hunting resources, such as online job databases and career software, and ideas for expanding your network using cutting-edge technology.

Chapter 6 helps you market yourself by creating a written pitch that'll survive a potential employer's "thirty-second countdown." I also offer techniques for creating bounce-back cover letters and résumés that meet the demands of scanning software and fax machines.

Of course, all job hunters meet with inevitable rejection, but in Chapter 7 I show you how easy it can be to create some wins along the way, too. I explain how informational interviewing can jumpstart a stalled job search and help you build an enduring network of professional allies.

The road to reemployment is paved with job interviews, and

Chapter 8 describes how to finesse even the toughest of them. You'll also find PIT-tested tips for deciding between multiple job offers and negotiating the best possible salary and benefits package.

In Appendix A, I reveal the top ten innovative job search tactics that have helped PIT members and others become gainfully—and happily—reemployed. Tactics range from printing a business card that can function as a mini-résumé to keeping a daily job-hunting journal.

Finally, our PIT library overflows with resources that we consider critical for professionals in transition, including career books, directories, periodicals, and CDs. I've listed them in Appendix B.

If you're currently in flux because you've lost your job, are underemployed, or sense change on the horizon, this book gives you a framework for achieving recovery and finding career success. My greatest hope is that after reading it, you'll learn how to turn your plight into positive action through knowledge and persistence.

Most important, I hope you'll have the opportunity to discover that there is life after unemployment. Hundreds of PITAs have proved it. As they can attest, unemployment is a temporary condition, not a disease!

CHAPTER 1

A Bridge Is a Terrible Thing to Burn

Parting Company Productively with Your Employer and Colleagues

You have just two hours to complete the week's business analysis, and you really could use another eight. The last thing you need on a Friday afternoon is a surprise meeting with your boss, Jerry, who has a penchant for harping on petty or irrelevant details at all the wrong times. As you close his office door, Jerry's nervous, pale, and guilt-ridden face hints that this won't be another of his famous "coaching and counseling" sessions. Your worries about the deadline evaporate as Jerry announces that the company is downsizing and must "flatten" the middle-management level...and, unfortunately, your position has been eliminated. You keep waiting for Jerry to yell, "Just kidding—April Fool's!" But you find nothing except the blank stare of an automaton. He mumbles how sorry he is, how difficult this has been for him, that downsizing is just a part of corporate life, and you'll probably be better off in the long run. You feel a lump in your throat as shock, fear, and anger course through your body.

Stunned and totally speechless, you now face a professional moment of truth. You have a major, split-second choice to make; you can exit stage left in either of two ways. One, you can enjoy a brief moment of vindication by telling Jerry exactly what you think of him and the company. Or two, you can deploy a positive leave-taking strategy that might later help you along your career path in ways you cannot now imagine. Choosing the latter is hard to fathom when you're in the thick of an unwanted departure, but it's still the best way to ensure that your encounter with unemployment is as brief as possible and that your professional reputation remains untarnished.

Pink Slips for All

Like death and taxes, job loss is inevitable at some point in your career. It's estimated that today's typical forty-year-old white-collar worker will change jobs two or three times during the remainder of his or her career, at least once involuntarily. Unemployment has become the great equalizer. These days, everyone in the workplace, even a top-salaried CEO, is vulnerable to layoff or termination. In fact, downsizing personnel right to the "irreducible core" is the key to corporate survival these days, and in many cases, even the top brass gets the old heave-ho. Sure, CEOs might leave with severance packages and golden parachutes, but they face the same emotions that we all do as we are stripped of the pursuit that gives so much meaning to our day-to-day existence and provides hope for the future of our families.

The Day of Reckoning

How will you cope with sudden job loss when it happens? The key is R&R: *restrain* and *remember*. Restrain your emotions, and remember the difference between what you can and can't control. You can't force your boss to rescind your termination, but you *can* hope to

part company responsibly and in a manner that benefits all parties. Word about your termination—and your subsequent actions—will travel quickly through the grapevine. Therefore, what you do now will very likely determine how you're perceived in the business community for years to come.

Someday you might run into a former colleague at another company. Or, if you choose to start your own business instead of getting another job, you might find yourself approaching your ex-employer about his or her becoming your first client. (Many entrepreneurs find this a great way to launch their businesses.) In short, why blemish your reputation as a professional and good corporate citizen for one brief moment of superficial gratification?

So, how can you create a sound psychological context for parting company well? Treat your impending severance as a "honeymoon in reverse." When you were hired, you enthusiastically geared up to become part of the corporate culture, meet new people, and immerse yourself in burgeoning, exciting projects. Now, as you leave your job, put the same tape in the machine, but play it backward. Gradually remove yourself from the job. Since you have limited time to disengage yourself from the people around you and from your work, your task is to gently shut one door after another as you distance yourself from the company and, finally, establish closure.

PIT TRAP: Don't let your negative feelings prevent you from leaving the company with your dignity and reputation intact.

Negotiating Again

There's another similarity between leaving and joining the company. Surprisingly, when you learn that you've been terminated, you're often in as strong a position to barter with your employer as you were when you were hired. Before you accepted employment, the company was anxious to create a desirable environment and bring you into the fold. Now, as your relationship with the business ends, your employer may be eager to help you bring your mutual association to a dignified close, because it will make his or her unpleasant chore easier.

Of course, your "severance leverage" depends in large part on the organization you're leaving. We've all heard of the mass layoffs in which the company passes out pink slips, engages security personnel to accompany people to their cubicles to clear out their desks, and then ushers ex-employees out the door all within twenty minutes. Even an employer who doesn't use such Draconian actions may have severance policies seemingly set in stone and expect you to take what you're offered without a murmur.

But the most rigid of companies can bend rules for individuals under certain circumstances. This happens more often than might be expected. Employees who were high-ranking or valued members of the team might negotiate a stronger package by reviewing the details of the severance agreement that is offered, taking it home to read carefully *before* deciding whether to sign it as it is. An employer might also selectively increase termination benefits to individual employees who can demonstrate the need. Smart employers know that a terminated employee treated well is less likely to turn into a problematic former employee.

If your employer wants you out the door badly enough, and it would please him or her to have you leave amicably and without stirring up the waters, you just might have some bargaining power, no matter what the company's policies. Ask not, get not. Unless you request it, you'll seldom receive anything above and beyond what your employer initially hands you, so it's up to you to take the initiative and name your terms. What do you have to lose?

PIT TRAP: Don't sign anything until you've had a chance to digest it.

When and How You Leave

Your employer would probably like to see you leave as soon as possible. But depending on the circumstances, you sometimes can create your own timetable and negotiate for a limited amount of time to get your affairs in order. This allows you to remain on the company payroll a bit longer, and it buys you time to contemplate your next career move.

One way to delay your exit date is to explain that it will take a certain number of days or weeks to finish whatever project you're working on, to hand off your duties to coworkers, or (as painful as it might be for you) to train your successor. Even if you can't talk your employer into extending your tenure at the company, you might not have to clean out your desk and leave in the presence of colleagues and coworkers. Instead, you can request permission to pack up your belongings on an appointed evening, weekend, or any time when you are unlikely to run into other employees. In turn, you might agree to let a security guard or manager accompany you to make sure you take only the items that rightfully belong to you.

Severance Package

Now that the when and how of your departure are agreed upon, it's time to answer the larger question: What will you get in return for your years of loyal service to the company and for parting on relatively good terms? Your employer may use a preset formula to determine the amount of severance pay it's willing to part with. For example, you might get a week's salary for every year you've been with the company. Nevertheless, if the employer sees you as a special case, you might just be able to get past the usual policy. Your employer might reward your years of dedicated service to the company if you ask for what you deserve. (Remember, if you don't ask for what you want, you certainly won't get it.) If it's impossible to bypass the formula, then you might have room to bargain for other privileges and perks that would help you feel more financially secure.

PIT members have successfully bargained with their employers for:

■ Several extra weeks of vacation pay (remember that you are already legally entitled to be paid for any vacation you have not taken).
■ The opportunity to apply for other jobs within the company
■ Permission to use the company's resources—such as the office, the photocopier, and a computer—to hunt for another job.
■ Payment for additional training.

If outplacement support wasn't part of the proposed severance package, you might ask the company to assist you in finding a new job. If you have been offered outplacement support, you can ask that it be open-ended, that is, the support will last until you've found another job, regardless of how long that takes.

On the other hand, your company might have a severance pay policy that depends on your rank in the company, or on the whims of your employer. In that case, there's no reason why you should jump at the parting package your employer initially proposes, any more than you had to accept whatever salary your employer first suggested when he or she first offered you the job. I can't stress enough that the money and perks are available for you—if you speak up.

When your employer describes your severance package for the first time, respond by thanking him or her. Then politely ask for the proposal in writing, and say that you'd like another week to review your financial position. Make sure your employer signs the proposal so there can be no dispute later. After you've had a chance to assess your needs, offer a counterproposal. You just might be surprised to find that you and your employer can come to terms on *your* terms. Whatever the outcome, it never hurts to try.

Health Insurance

No one can afford to be uninsured. Fortunately, you probably won't have to either, despite your termination. Legally, you are almost certainly entitled to continued health insurance coverage under your company's group plan. Make sure you thoroughly discuss and understand your company's health care benefits and how long you will qualify for them once the severance period begins. In addition, be sure to discuss COBRA (Consolidated Omnibus Budget Reconciliation Act of 1986) benefits. You may not know that COBRA requires most employers to offer departing employees continued group health insurance benefits.* If you're like most people, you're entitled to the same health insurance benefits you had at your company's group rate, plus a two percent management fee, for eighteen months after your termination date. However, you'll be paying 100 percent of the premiums, and that may dramatically increase your cost for the same level of health care coverage. The costs might be lower if you join another group insurance policy, so it pays to shop around for your own coverage if you'll be paying the insurance premiums. (If you have a pre-existing medical condition, however, that can make it difficult for you to find another insurance carrier.) Check with professional associations and recreational clubs to which you belong; they often offer members discounted coverage.

As employee-friendly (if not cost-effective) as COBRA may be, be aware it doesn't cover everyone all the time. The law doesn't apply to churches and the federal government, although the latter's employees are covered by the Federal Employee Health Benefits Act of 1988, which is similar to COBRA. Also, if you were dismissed due to "willful misconduct," you're not entitled to COBRA's protection.

Note, too, that COBRA only applies to health coverage, that is, medical, dental, and vision insurance. It doesn't cover group life and long-term disability insurance. You might, however, negotiate with your employer to continue these insurance policies, if you had them, under the same terms as your health coverage. Also, your employer might consider striking a deal with you regarding the cost of your health insurance coverage. For example, perhaps the company will

* You can write to the U.S. Department of Labor, Pension and Welfare Benefits Administration, Division of Technical Assistance and Inquiries, 200 Constitution Ave., NW, Room N-5658, Washington, DC 20210, or call (202) 219-8776 to get information about COBRA.

continue to pay all or part of your monthly insurance fees for an agreed-upon period, say, eighteen months or until you're covered under a new employer's group plan, whichever comes first.

PIT TRAP: If you assume that COBRA is your only health care option, you may end up paying too much for your insurance.

Getting Legal Help

When all else fails, you can engage a labor attorney to advocate for your rights. Although you can consult with a lawyer at any time during the termination process, you immediately change the dynamics of the situation if you officially bring an attorney in to advocate for your rights. You might get a better deal by hiring a labor attorney, but you also reduce your chances of parting on good terms with your employer. That said, there are still times when you need legal representation. If your employer is denying you the benefits to which you're entitled under the law, if you feel you've been discriminated against, or if you've been wrongly terminated, it's time to sacrifice your relationship with your employer and call in a hired legal gun to do your bidding and protect your rights.

Seeking legal assistance means investing time and money, but in exchange, you'll get:

■ **Perspective**. An uninvolved professional lets you know what you can realistically negotiate from your former employer.
■ **Peace of mind**. If your severance agreement is fair and appropriate, you may not need to take further action. You can sign the severance agreement (and thereby relinquish all legal recourse) or develop a renegotiation strategy.
■ **Guidance**. You learn about the appropriate next steps to take before you commit to a course of action.

Finally, a labor attorney can also help you level the playing field;

at a time when you're overwhelmed by emotions, you'd do well to have a clear-thinking professional on your side. So how do you find the right labor attorney for your needs? You can:

- Check with your state bar association.
- Find out who your company's legal counsel is and go to that firm's competitor.
- Ask friends and acquaintances for their recommendations.

Being a nice guy is inappropriate when your company's treatment of you violates the law. It pays to facilitate your settlement with the help of a legal advocate.

Spinning Your Story

Whether you exit alone or bring in a lawyer, you still have one foot out the door. Therefore, you'll soon have need for a viable, face-saving explanation of why you left the company. The unvarnished truth is always important, but how you position your departure story is vital. You and your employer must agree to an explanation for your termination that everyone can live with.

Even if you are leaving your job under duress, there are still countless ways of framing your reasons for departing, and some will benefit you far more than others. You want your colleagues, associates, vendors, and potential future employers to hear whatever version of the story shows you in your best light. For example, "My position was eliminated due to downsizing" sounds better than "My boss had to cut one salary from the budget, and mine was it"; "My department is undergoing some managerial changes" has a better ring to it than "My new supervisor let me go because she and I had a personality conflict." Other face-saving scenarios include "I've decided to redirect my career"; "The projects I was working on were phased out"; or "My manager and I had differences in our workstyles,"—all of which beat "I was sacked" hands down.

Once you've established a simple, plausible explanation for your leave taking, ask your employer to agree to it. Your employer may want to tweak your story, but your explanations should jibe in any case. This may well be your final opportunity to negotiate with your employer, and it shouldn't be too difficult. Even the most belligerent boss will hesitate to make your leave taking more painful than it has to be or to sabotage your chances of reemployment. Also, employers won't want to hurt your job prospects for fear they'll find themselves vulnerable to a lawsuit.

PIT TRICK: Don't worry about saving face for the company. As you spin a termination story, concentrate on your own reputation.

Taking Care of Business

Just as you don't want to erupt emotionally as you prepare to leave the company, you can't afford to let your job performance slide either. You may be tempted to put in the minimum of effort while the clock ticks to your departure—that's only natural. But it won't benefit you in the long run. You've worked hard to earn a reputation as a conscientious and competent employee, and there's no reason for you to be remembered as anything less.

Also, you've put a lot of energy into your work and given it your heart and soul. You probably won't be around now to see all of the projects you began come to fruition, but you can still take pride in contributing your best efforts during your remaining time at the company.

Taking It with You

It isn't always convenient, comfortable, or even possible to close out your workspace once you walk out the door for the last time. So make a list of everything you want to pack up and carry home. What you want to take, though, may not always be what you're *allowed* to take. You can't take the company's property. For example, a stapler that your employer paid for stays with the company, even if you have been its sole user for the better part of a decade. Other items, such as your Rolodex, may belong to you, and you *can* take your belongings with you—usually depending on how they relate to your job, how you plan to use them, and whether you signed an employee agreement before you joined the company.

If, for instance, you were a salesperson, you might not be able to take a list of customers because you could end up selling them a competing company's widgets in the future. However, it might be perfectly acceptable for an accountant to take the same list of customers and use it to, say, keep in touch during the holidays. Unless there's a security guard hovering over you as you pack, you'll probably find yourself running into some gray areas—that is, items that belong to you but that your company would prefer to hold onto anyway. In those cases, it becomes a judgment call, and you'll have to decide what to take and what to leave behind based on your sense of ethics. Alternatively, you can consult your attorney.

The choice might be taken out of your hands if you signed an employee agreement at hiring. This contract probably compels you to leave behind proprietary information and may prevent you from competing professionally with your employer for a certain length of time. Even if you signed such an agreement, though, it might not hold up in court. Don't automatically assume that something you'd like to take is off-limits because of an employee agreement you've signed. Discuss it with your attorney before you jump to conclusions.

In any case, you want to take items (or photocopies, if the originals are unavailable to you) that will help you when it's time to seek another job as long as your taking them poses no threat to your company. Make sure to pack:

■ Samples of your best work.
■ Letters of praise you've received from customers, clients, etc.
■ Performance evaluations.

Pack anything else that could be of use to you down the road. And while making a packing list and checking it twice, remember to lock down any benefits to which you are entitled (profit sharing, 401(k), pension benefits, stock options, etc.). Have your employer explain, in a signed letter to you, how you will receive any monies or securities. Will the funds be paid outright, or rolled over and disbursed to you on a certain date? How will vested stock options be handled? It's up to you, and you alone, to make sure you're properly compensated for your service to the company.

PIT TRICK: Make a packing list in advance so you'll remember to take what's most important when you leave the company.

Saying a Proper Farewell

While you're tying up logistical and financial loose ends, you also need to consider personal relationships. During your time with the company, you've been part of a professional network that may have included colleagues, associates, vendors, customers, clients, and the public. Now you have to find a way to say goodbye to the members of your network, and it probably won't be easy for any of you.

The first step in easing the pain is to pre-empt the information flow. That is, try to be the bearer of the news yourself, even if it means putting on your running shoes to beat the grapevine and the rumor mill. Also, be sure to tell everyone the same story—preferably the one that you and your employer have agreed upon in advance—about why you're leaving the company. Fight the natural urge to blast the boss or trash the company. Doing so may make you feel better, but it doesn't make your situation any better, and it *could* make things much worse.

In some cases, your employer might ask you to delay telling people about your impending departure, particularly if you're in the process of closing an important deal with a third party. Comply with your employer's wishes, both to keep the peace and to benefit the company. Similarly, you may be forced to leave the company before you've had a chance to say goodbye to your coworkers and the other members of your network. In either case, you still can ease the blow and put a positive spin on your departure if you take the reins. PIT members who had already left their organizations still orchestrated gracious exits after the fact by making phone calls and sending letters of farewell to everyone on their address lists. Their message was: "It's been a great eight years. As you know, I'm moving on to bigger and better things. I've really appreciated the opportunity to work with you." You can do the same.

By recognizing people who have helped you in the past, you're creating an important bridge that will serve you well in the future. You never know who will be able to help you jump-start your career when you're ready. A call or letter from you gives your contacts a reason to get in touch and provides you with an easier entrée to them when the time is right to reconnect.

PIT TRICK: Take the time to thank people who helped you along the way; they just might be the key to your future success.

Relationships After Termination

Many of your closest contacts inevitably treat you differently once you've broken the bad news to them. No matter how close with you they've been, few people want to attach themselves to a "lame duck." Now that you're leaving the company, people may not run to you with their questions because you no longer have all the answers or the authority you once had. Some colleagues may treat you as though you're a victim of the plague and keep their distance for fear of catching the "pink slip disease." Others, who feel guilty for "surviving," may also avoid you. Whatever the reasons, your coworkers' withdrawal won't necessarily turn your last days and weeks on the job into a nightmare if you deal with it openly and head on.

First, understand how your leaving affects your colleagues. You may be leaving them to cope with a heavier workload or muddle through complicated projects on their own or deal with a new political landscape in the workplace. As your colleagues' feelings about your termination undoubtedly mirror your own, encourage them to talk about their feelings with you. Begin to work together through the shock, anger, sadness, fear, and other emotions related to job loss.

Remember and share PIT's motto: *Unemployment is a temporary condition, not a disease.* Exude confidence both in your own ability to bounce back from unemployment and in your colleagues' capacity to go on without you. As much as possible, focus on the positive aspects of your experience in working together, and emphasize the ways in which your colleagues have helped you grow as a professional, as well as how much you've appreciated their support.

Alas, however you handle yourself during your final days on your job, your coworkers inevitably begin to withdraw from you both professionally and emotionally. Like it or not, they have to move on with their lives, and they expect you to do the same. If they give you the "cold shoulder," don't take it personally. Instead, accept it as dispassionately as you can. Understand that you're not losing friends; you're simply getting a clearer understanding of the difference between friends and colleagues. Consider the knowledge you gain to be a perk of your termination.

PIT TRAP: However distant your colleagues suddenly may seem, don't be afraid to remind them that you'll soon be leaving the company. That enables you to tie up loose ends and allows everyone to achieve closure.

Gathering References

A final leave-taking responsibility entails rounding up your potential references. Regardless of how great your merit or popularity, never make the mistake of expecting anyone to provide a reference. Many companies mandate that your manager, personnel department, and coworkers only verify your name, job title, and how long you were with the company instead of providing you with actual references. A "nonreference" like this doesn't help your cause, but you're on shaky ground if you ask colleagues to risk their jobs by violating company policy.

An alternative is to ask potential references to provide letters of recommendation to potential employers. Provide a sample letter, and ask your references to write one for you that relates a similar message. Be aware, though, that employers are usually wary of form letters, so you might want to request that your references agree to provide a personalized note written to prospective employers as needed during the job campaign.

Colleagues might also be willing to provide their home phone numbers so that potential employers can talk to them privately. But don't expect too much from those who remain behind while you leave. As I've stressed, you're a part of the company's past, and what you do with your future is strictly up to you—no one else bears any responsibility for it.

PIT TRAP: Never expect references, even from your most valued colleagues; be prepared for your associates to follow company policies that prohibit such support.

Unemployment Compensation

Until now, I've talked about how to gently close the corporate doors behind you, tie up loose ends, and make a gracious exit from the company. Once your job officially ends, there's another critical matter you have to take care of as soon as possible: filing a claim for unemployment compensation.

If you don't like to accept governmental handouts, be assured that collecting unemployment compensation falls into a very different category. Your employer kicked monies into the insurance pot while you were working. As a result, you're entitled to the unemployment benefits that can help you sustain yourself and your family once your paychecks stop, until you get back on your feet.

You won't be able to collect your first compensation check until two weeks after your termination date, and only then after you've run through your severance and vacation pay. Nevertheless, you should file a claim with your local unemployment office *as soon as your job ends* so that the payments can begin on time. When you file, you meet with an unemployment counselor who wants to know, among other things, why you've been terminated from your job. This is a good opportunity to use the story that your employer and you agreed to tell; if your version of the facts closely matches your employer's, your claim should be processed smoothly and painlessly. Note that even if you and your employer agree that yours is a mutually agreed upon separation instead of a dismissal, you're still eligible to collect unemployment compensation. You are unable to collect unemployment compensation only if you:

■ Were fired due to willful misconduct.
■ Committed a felony.
■ Quit.

PIT TRICK: Apply for unemployment as soon as possible; you'll be able to use the unemployment office's job-hunting resources as soon as you register.

Action Plan Recap

You may be out of a job, but that doesn't mean you have to be out of control of the situation. The following checklist helps you organize your actions from the time when you're informed of your termination until you officially walk out the front door for the last time.

❒ Decide on a termination date.
❒ Agree on when you'll pack your personal belongings.
❒ Negotiate a severance package.

❐ Get your severance package offer in writing.
❐ Sign up for COBRA or other health insurance benefits.
❐ Secure legal representation, if you need it.
❐ Get your employer's agreement to your termination story.
❐ Tie up loose ends professionally.
❐ Make a packing list.
❐ Lock in your benefits.
❐ Gather references.
❐ Apply for unemployment compensation.
❐ Say goodbye.

You've probably been a team player for so long that it is almost impossible to imagine how you'll function on your own. If you plan ahead, however, you can leave the company with your dignity, self-esteem, and security intact. You can leave in a state of well-being, too, knowing that you've secured your immediate future as much as possible and have built some strong bridges. Once you've dealt with the initial challenges of separation, it's time to face a tidal wave of emotions that come with losing your job. The following chapter explains what lies ahead as the next stage of your life unfolds.

CHAPTER 2

The Stark Truth About Job Loss

Understanding the Process of Transition

Three months have passed since you were laid off. Other people in your position might have panicked or felt sorry for themselves, but not you. You confidently picked up the phone and called everyone you knew, convinced that one of your contacts would offer you a position or at least steer you toward a job opportunity, and that before you knew it, you'd be back at work. In the meantime, you had no time for self-pity and learned to live with constant mood swings. Something would break soon, and you could hold it all together until it did.

Despite your optimism and indefatigable spirit, the "job savior" seems to have ignored your existence. Professional colleagues who were eager to talk to you in the past either aren't returning your calls or have little to say to you. Reality is beginning to sink in: You could be in for a long siege of unemployment. Meanwhile, you have bills to pay, and the pressure is mounting; more and more, it's becoming a struggle to keep your feelings inside, and you're afraid the lid will blow off.

Just how many setbacks are you supposed to endure without breaking?

What if you drop your guard and let your emotions run free—how will you ever be able to get on with the business of looking for a job?

Life After Unemployment

There's no denying it: Losing your job is a life-changing event. Your professional career has been taken away from you and, just as surely as if you'd lost a loved one, you need time to grieve. Through my work with PIT members and with the help of Dr. Elisabeth Kübler-Ross, the renowned expert on death and dying, I've identified what I call the "emotional wave" (or e-wave for short), which represents the job-loss grief process.

Along with the emotional issues you are likely to encounter when you're unemployed, there are also physical and behavioral symptoms of job loss. PIT members often cite loss of appetite, problems falling asleep at night, forgetfulness, difficulty concentrating, anxiety attacks, and migraine headaches as common reactions to coping with job loss. Additional reactions may include dizziness, palpitations, forgetfulness, aching limbs, hyperventilating, perspiring, repetitive dreams, inordinate risk taking, endless chattering, irritability, and hyperactivity. It is also very common to feel out of sync with the world and out of control. There's often some interplay between the emotional, physical, and behavioral symptoms of job loss. For example, recurring nightmares might trigger feelings of humiliation and depression, while fear and panic might cause dizziness, palpitations, or perspiring. Actual physical and behavioral manifestations of unemployment vary widely from one person to another, but the e-wave typically unfolds in the context of at least some of these symptoms.

The Emotional Wave of Unemployment

Here's an overview of how the e-wave works. When you get the news that you've been terminated, this sudden change in your life pitches you into an ocean of emotion. As you tumble from wave to wave, you experience shock and denial, fear and panic, anger, bargaining, depression, and temporary acceptance. Just when you think you've reached the trough of the wave, you begin to climb up to the crest of another wave. The cycle continues until you learn to positively channel, rather than avoid, your real feelings. Once you're able to confront and manage your e-wave emotions, you can navigate your way through the stormy waters and, eventually, safely reach the other shore.

Working through the stages of death and dying is a somewhat linear experience. Death is an ending, one that produces built-in closure because of the socially acceptable rituals that are associated with it. Family and friends provide empathy and support. There may be a memorial service, wake, shiva, or other custom that honors the deceased and closes the circle of life. Sharing memories and emotions together in safe space is an integral part of the grieving process.

Contrast this with the trauma of losing your job, where there are no socially acceptable rituals or channels through which to process job loss. The rawness of your emotions can become part of an endless loop. Even after you've experienced all the stages of job-loss grief and you feel ready to move on with your career, a setback might send you plummeting into the depths of despair again. This explains why the final stage of acceptance in bereavement becomes temporary acceptance in the e-wave.

Although job-loss grief is a universal experience, there are minor differences in how individuals experience it. In that way, it's similar to bereavement. You might pass through all of its stages in sequence, or you might bypass one stage and jump directly to another. You could even experience the e-wave stages in a different order from how most people do. Sometimes it might take you weeks to cycle through the e-wave stages, while at other times you experience them all in the space of five minutes.

Once you understand the e-wave, you can predict how it might shape the weeks ahead of you and prepare to deal effectively with each emotional stage, as you encounter it. This is the first step toward interrupting the cycle, reestablishing control of your life, and ultimately achieving reemployment. This chapter examines each of the e-wave stages in detail, introduces you to PIT members who have survived them, and provides proven strategies for overcoming the challenges the stages present.

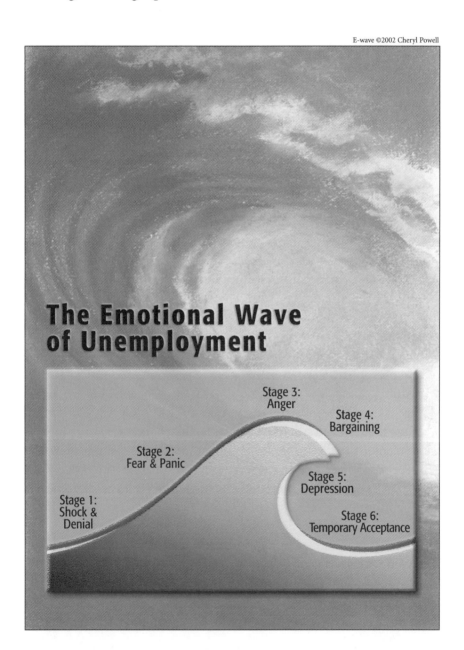

Stage One: Shock and Denial

Julie had been the director of marketing for a major catalog company for only four months when she learned her job was being eliminated. She recalls her immediate reaction to the news: "It was like somebody punched me in the stomach. It really knocked the wind out of me…I couldn't breathe."

Like so many people who have just been terminated, Julie's first response was utter disbelief. She heard what her vice-president said about company-wide layoffs and expressed appropriate dismay; but deep inside, where it counted, she didn't believe a word of it. Even as she went through the motions of packing her belongings, saying goodbye to her colleagues, and leaving the office, she was thoroughly convinced she'd awaken at any moment from her nightmare and things would be just fine.

You might react to the news of your termination stoically, bravely, or tearfully. Whatever your response, thoughts like these are likely to engulf you:

- How could this have happened to me?
- It must be a mistake.
- It's the end of the world.
- My life is over.
- What will I tell my spouse and children?

Whatever the specifics, thoughts of this nature are likely to race through your mind as you get the bad news. The announcement of your termination doesn't seem quite real, and at the time, nothing else does, either. You feel detached, as if you are watching yourself and the world around you in a movie. During this stage, people often say that they're "blown away," or they've "zoned out." In short, your mind shuts down to protect you. Although you may feel you've been punched in the stomach, the full impact of your termination may not hit you for days, weeks, or however long it takes for the reality of your job loss to sink in.

Coping with Shock and Denial

"In the beginning, all I wanted to do was curl up into a ball and go to sleep," recalls Laura, an out-of-work senior marketing manager who instinctively had the right idea. When people ask me what to do while they're going through the shock-and-denial stage of the e-wave, I advise them to do just what Laura felt like doing: nothing.

Give yourself the time and privacy needed to recuperate. This isn't the moment to write letters, call people, or broadcast the news of your termination to the world (the only exception is your family; see Chapter 3). If you go off like a loose cannon and try to find another job before you've had time to sit alone and begin to adjust to your termination, everyone sees the trauma of unemployment in your eyes and hears it in your voice. It's perfectly normal to come unglued. Just don't do it around the people whose help you'll need down the road when you begin your job search.

PIT TRICK: Take as much time as you need to recuperate from the shock of unemployment before you start spreading the news.

Stage 2: Fear and Panic

John, a former merchandising manager, describes how vulnerable he felt when his shock and denial dissipated and he entered the next stage of the e-wave. "I bought bolt locks for my home and had an alarm installed on my car. It seemed like everyone, everywhere I went, was looking at me. I was always looking over my shoulder, waiting for the next personal disaster to occur. It was like constantly sitting in an electric chair and waiting to be zapped again and again, without warning."

Once the first numbness wears off, fear and panic are likely to take over your thoughts. Because you've suffered a setback in your professional life, you may feel extremely vulnerable. Many PIT members experience overwhelming dread as insignificant events suddenly trigger fear or panic.

Tom, an aerospace engineer, explains how he obsessed about the heater in his house while he was out of work. "Whenever the furnace blower came on, I thought of the expense. How long will the furnace run, I wondered, and how much will it cost?" Tom never even gave his heating expenses a thought while he was employed, and now they haunted him.

Unemployment certainly brings with it a host of valid concerns. But during the fear-and-panic stage of the e-wave, it is common to spend much of your time and energy catastrophizing about such issues as:

- What if I have to declare bankruptcy?
- Will I lose everything I own?
- Will my family and friends abandon me?
- Is this the end of my career?
- Will I ever find a job as good as the one I lost?

Fear and panic may also lead to indecisiveness. Every choice takes on exaggerated importance, and you may feel as though the world will end if you make the wrong decision. For example, Jay, who lost his job as a software engineer, remembers how much of an ordeal it was for him to get up in the morning and figure out what to wear each day. "Nothing seemed to look right…I'd change my tie ten times, and then go back to the one I had on originally." Each time he hesitated, Jay felt as though his indecision only proved he was a loser, and of course that made it even tougher for him to trust his own instincts.

Panic and indecision are appropriate responses to losing your job. Nothing could be more natural than to feel a tremendous sense of violation and fear because your livelihood has just been snatched away for no good reason, and you don't know what tomorrow will bring. However, it is important to understand that uncontrolled and disproportionate fright can quickly drain your time and energy— and immobilize you, if you let it.

Coping with Fear and Panic

The key both to minimizing and surviving fear and panic is to put your concerns back into perspective. Denying or repressing your worries doesn't work, but neither does agonizing about them incessantly. So confront your fears on a reasonable timetable. Give yourself a "worry period"—say, fifteen minutes—each day, and restrict your worrying to that time slot. If you catch yourself slipping up and fretting about the future outside of the designated time slot, stop. Make an "appointment" to deal with it later, during your sanctioned worrying time.

Another fear-halting strategy is to list your worries on a sheet of paper. Write down every gloomy unemployment scenario you can think of, from "I'll never find another job as long as I live" to "My spouse will divorce me, and I'll be left all alone." Then, when you've committed all your fears to paper, decide which ones have a basis in reality and which others you can instantly dismiss. Strike the latter, which undoubtedly include most of your what-if worries. You then have a set of reasonable concerns that you can *prioritize* and *address*.

If you're having trouble making decisions, limit the time you give yourself to choose. Give yourself, say, two minutes to make an *A/B* choice—such as should you or shouldn't you make a phone call—and then stick with your decision. Take a step back from the problem, if you can, and consider it. You'll probably find that few choices you make are of the forever variety. In all likelihood, you'll get a chance to rectify any mistakes you happen to make, so it's okay to forge a-head for now.

Stage 3: Anger

When Diane lost her job as a lab assistant, she reports, "People would-n't return my phone calls or respond to my letters. One time, I went to a grocery store and saw a former associate walking down the aisle beside me. For an instant, our eyes met, and then she raced ahead without acknowledging me and ducked into another aisle. It was as though I'd suddenly become a plague victim, and no one would come near me." Diane was furious. "All I wanted to do was even the score with everyone, from my former associate to my next-door neighbor who'd stopped making eye contact with me. I just needed for everyone to know how it felt, but no one seemed to care."

Once fear and panic have run their course, it is common to begin to fume about all that has been taken away. Common thoughts include:

- This isn't fair.
- How can they do this to me?
- This is an outrage.
- They have no right.
- How would *they* like it?
- They can't imagine how I feel.
- They're rude and insensitive.
- How can I get through to them?

Because there's no specific person at whom you can vent your rage, the anger accumulates inside of you. You stew in your own juices, as it were. Your anger gets your heart beating, head thumping, and adrenaline flowing. You can't sit still or you'll explode. You want action *now*. It would feel great to reach out and throttle someone. Revenge dominates your thinking. You want to knock others out of their routines, wipe the smug looks off their faces, and spread the agony.

Of course, you shouldn't give in to your anger. But you can use it. Anger is fire in your belly. It's righteous indignation. And it can energize you. Properly channeled, anger makes the difference between success and failure in your job search. You can channel your anger to propel yourself into positive activities that lead to reemployment when the time is right.

But the flip side is that if you let your anger fester, it overwhelms and immobilizes you. You'll be not only unemployable but impossible to live with or near. All you get in return for your anger is alienation, which leads to more fury, and the cycle continues. To break out of this e-wave stage and, ultimately, get past the trauma of unemployment, you have to work through your anger…and forgive.

Coping with Anger

"If you want a stain out, *shout* it out," extolled the old laundry detergent commercial. Shouting in an appropriate setting—say, inside your basement or garage when no one else is around—is an appropriate way of exhausting your anger. Your body freely translates your emotions into physical actions, so why not take advantage of it? There's never been a better time to install a punching bag in your spare room, put on the gloves, and go about the business of getting into peak physical condition. Alternatively, you can walk, run, or go to the soccer field and kick goals until you're exhausted. Other people report that kneading bread dough, beating sofa cushions, or throwing pillows helps them vent.

When I needed to burn off my anger at losing my job, I wholeheartedly embraced an assignment from my mother-in-law, who needed an electrical line installed. My task was to dig a hundred-foot trench and bury the cable. You know something? It felt great! If Mom hadn't needed my help, I would have shoveled concrete, dug a well in my backyard, or done anything that would make me sweat until I dropped. Whatever you can do without hurting yourself or anyone else is appropriate.

But that doesn't mean you won't fantasize about ways of evening the score with your former employer. To work through the frustration harmlessly, you might throw darts at a board overlaid with a picture of your supervisor until you're worn out. What you *shouldn't* do with your rage is suck it in, or blow it out at the wrong times or in the wrong places. Avoid the temptation to blast your boss or former employer in professional settings, such as during interviews or networking sessions, because an angry person is—rightfully—perceived as unemployable.

According to Lynne McClure, author of *Risky Business: Managing Employee Violence in the Workplace* (Haworth Publishing), the worst thing you can do with your anger is pretend it's not there. McClure stresses that if you don't recognize your anger, you can't deal with it and you can't heal. "When you see someone who was fired and becomes violent as a result, you're looking at someone who's stuck at the anger stage." Although McClure believes job-loss anger is natural, she emphasizes that the anger should ebb and flow and, finally, disappear. She cautions, "If the anger is constant and you're fixated on it, then you're ready for therapy."

Stage 4: Bargaining

Once you're done gnashing your teeth, and you've run ten miles and dug the trench, you're exhausted. Your mind goes blank. The desire to fight and get revenge disappears. Instead, you convince yourself that now something or someone is going to come along to save you, if only you prove yourself worthy. Thoughts like the following occur to you:

- Maybe it was all a mistake.
- Maybe they'll apologize and take me back.
- The situation can't be as bad as it seems.
- I'll get another job right away.
- I'm due for something good to happen.

You promise yourself that if your boss rehires you or you get another job, you'll never take home another company-bought pencil. You'll gladly work ten hours a day, six days a week, without complaint. You'll never take a paycheck for granted again. Once the money starts coming in, you'll start a savings account, a retirement plan, and a college fund for your kids. You'll learn from your past mistakes. You'll become the worthiest employee, family member, and world citizen who ever was.

You may also begin to believe that a painless ending to your unemployment crisis is right around the corner. "I'm sure my buddy Bob will keep his word and help me find a job, because I'm a good person," you tell yourself. "If only the director of human resources at the ABC company will call me, then I'll get a job." "All I have to do is learn the latest software program, and my phone will ring off the hook."

In your attempt to make the pain go away, you may invent a "job savior." This is the person or event who will make everything okay. PIT member Scott explains how he looked for his job savior at a trade show soon after he lost his job in sales. "People kept telling me what a good person I was and reassuring me that I'd have no problem finding a job. So I flew across the country to attend a trade show, where I handed out résumés like a paper boy. I'd say to every vendor I met, 'I just lost my job, can you help me out?' I was absolutely convinced my next employer was at the show, and someone would create the perfect job for me." After Scott had handed out two hundred résumés and sent fifty follow-up letters without netting a single interview, bitter disappointment engulfed him. However, he continued to believe there was someone out there who would eventually work a miracle and take away his pain. "It took me a long time to realize there was no job savior, and that it was my responsibility to find a job," Scott recalls.

Coping with Bargaining

No matter how much you might want to rely on fate, friends, or strangers to bail you out of the situation you're in, you have to accept the fact that *finding a job is your responsibility.* For example, suppose Sam told you that if you ever need anything, all you had to do was let him know. Now you're desperate to talk to him, and he won't return your calls. Or maybe your old college buddy is now very well connected, and if she'd only hook you up with her contacts, you'd have a job in no time. But mysteriously, she's always at a meeting when you try to reach her.

PIT member Pete sums up the reasons why there are no job saviors. "People would call, express concern and surprise about my job loss, and talk for a while. Then they were gone. They acted like their duty was over. It was like they'd gone to a funeral home, offered their condolences, and now they were ready to leave. They felt bad, but after they did their duty they wanted to go on with their lives. They wanted me to disappear, because being in touch with me was a reminder of their own vulnerability." If you're still expecting your old buddy to rescue you, investigate the reality of what you're telling yourself. You *will* find a job, of course—but it will happen through your own efforts, not those of a miracle worker.

Stage 5: Depression

After Alan had pounded the pavement for four months while he looked for a teaching job, he became convinced that his unemployment was a just punishment. "I blamed myself for being awkward, hesitant, and clumsy, and I relived every embarrassing mistake I'd ever made. Beating myself up seemed logical and reasonable. It was natural for me to play the martyr and feel sorry for myself. After a while, my self-inflicted pain actually began to feel good. It distracted me from my financial problems for awhile, anyway."

Once you realize that becoming the most deserving professional in the world won't get your old boss to reverse her decision to terminate you or inspire another employer to put you on his payroll, despair may set in. You may feel abandoned, as though everything you had—your routine, status, professional network, office, and even your coffee cup—has been taken away. So you decide you probably deserve to be where you are. Every nasty thing your spouse, in-laws, kids, neighbors, or colleagues ever said about you is probably true. Every skeleton in your closet, whatever mistakes you've made, and any unresolved issues from your past come back to haunt you. Some of the ideas that creep into your mind are:

- It's all my fault.
- I deserve to be unemployed.
- You had it coming, hotshot.
- They gave me enough rope, and I finally hung myself.
- If only I hadn't done that.
- I'm worthless.
- This is the end of the road for me.
- They finally discovered that I'm a fraud.

Depression is, in effect, anger turned inward. During my own bouts with depression while I was unemployed, I vividly imagined myself sitting on a park bench, unshaven. In my mind's eye, my clothes were tattered; I was holding a bottle of wine. My car had been repossessed. My wife and kids had left me to my misery. And I knew I deserved every bit of what was happening to me because I'd lost my job.

Many PIT members have woeful tales of unemployment. Eileen, for one, remembers when her depression hit. "All I wanted to do was sleep. I stopped answering the phone, didn't go outside, and basically gave up on life. People would knock on the door, and I wouldn't answer. I had no energy or desire to face my unemployment. I felt stupid, awkward, and ashamed for losing my job. I just wanted to hide and be left alone." Eileen felt that her world had ended. She was a loser and a coward, with nothing to live for, and nothing to do.

It's also common, while you're in the throes of depression, to hit bottom (in my case, I wrecked my car on the way to a job interview and landed in the hospital). You're in a downward spiral, and everything seems to go wrong simultaneously. When you reach the bottom of the pit, there's only one way you can go, and that's up. Unfortunately, hitting bottom isn't necessarily something that only happens *once* during your voyage through the e-wave. For some PIT members, it happens several times, and each time they have to deal with it as if they were on their first round. The good news is that there are proven techniques you can use to move from depression to action.

Coping with Depression

When depression takes over, you're flooded with feelings of worthlessness, guilt, and lethargy. It takes all your energy just to get out of bed in the morning, and there isn't much left for fighting your way out of the gloom. Yet that's exactly what you must do. If you give in to depression, you'll never get your job search into gear. You'll remain in limbo, licking your wounds, and hiding yourself away from the world and everyone in it. What you should do instead is follow some PIT-tested techniques for chasing away the e-wave doldrums.

Depression is a cloud that, among other things, blots out your good feelings about yourself. Lift the cloud by forgiving your past misdeeds. Pamper yourself. Indulge in a bubble bath, a walk in the woods, a ticket to the opera, or whatever makes you feel special. Do all the things you never had time to do. Play with your kids, and spend time with your spouse. Go to a comedy club or rent your favorite comic's videotapes; humor is another effective way to combat depression. Step outside your situation when you can, and laugh at it. Treat yourself as if you were your own best friend.

Do something productive and helpful for others. Volunteer to chaperone your child's field trip, serve food at a soup kitchen, clean up the litter in a local playground, raise funds for your favorite charity, or the like.

To combat the lethargy that depression often brings, exercise. Running, walking, swimming, and other aerobic activities give you energy. The goal isn't to beat your "personal best" score, log more miles than you ever have, or win a competition with anyone else. Rather, the idea is to let loose, shake off the blues, and do something nice for your mind and body. Also, exercising helps you sleep better, and you need your rest to keep yourself healthy enough to execute an effective job search.

Stage 6: Temporary Acceptance

At some point, the gloom recedes and you realize that it's time to move forward. Although the crisis of unemployment is still with you every moment of every day, you have some breathing room. You can think about where you've been, where you are, and where you're going. This is the e-wave stage when you're functioning at the highest level, and you can create an action plan. Some healthy concepts that begin to sink in are:

- The past is past.
- It's time to move on.

■ Sitting here on the sofa isn't doing me any good.

■ I can't change anything by kicking myself in the butt.

■ Why dwell on what I can't change?

■ My job search is my responsibility, and I can make it happen.

■ What I do with my future is up to me.

In the temporary acceptance stage, you pick yourself up by the bootstraps and get on with your life. You absolve yourself of blame for your unemployment and, at the same time, charge yourself with the responsibility for your career.

Coping with Temporary Acceptance

If temporary acceptance were the final stop on the journey to your recovery, there'd be nothing to cope with. It would be time to kick up your heels and celebrate. You'd be "over" the trauma of unemployment. But as I've pointed out, the e-wave is a cycle rather than a series of linear stages. You might accept your situation with resolve one day, and sink back into depression the next. One minute, you might be full of optimism, and the next, you might imagine yourself living on the street.

You'll frequently experience extreme mood swings for as long as you're unemployed. Also, while you're riding the e-wave, your feelings are exaggerated. The highs are higher, and the lows lower. Seemingly minor events—a rejection letter, a curt response to a phone call, or not being invited to a holiday celebration—can catapult you from the plateau of temporary acceptance to the depths of shock and denial, fear and panic, anger, bargaining, or depression.

Use the sanctuary of temporary acceptance to prepare yourself for what lies ahead. Develop a plan for snatching victory from the jaws of grief, and for finding equanimity and dignity in every stage as you cycle through your e-wave emotions. Most important, prepare yourself to face the working world again from a perspective of personal responsibility, forgiveness, and confidence.

Moving On

Even though most PIT members and other professionals I've worked with have cycled through the e-wave at least once on the way to reemployment, there's no hard-and-fast rule that says everyone has to suffer from prolonged job-loss grief. A job may fall into your lap before you've fully experienced the e-wave stages. In fact, your phone might be ringing as you read this, and the caller might be prepared to offer you a golden career opportunity. If that's the case, by all means, accept it. Don't worry that you might miss something or sabotage your chances for long-term happiness because you haven't suffered enough. However, in my experience, most people *do* find it necessary to work through the e-wave stages before they can successfully move on with their professional lives. They find, in fact, that dealing with the trauma of unemployment from a position of knowledge and anticipation is the key to getting their career back on track.

You should now have an idea of what to expect while you're riding the e-wave of unemployment. In the next chapter, we take a look at what your family members are likely to experience during this time. You learn how to help them work through their experiences, and how the trauma of unemployment ultimately can bring your family even closer together.

Home and Hearth

Guiding Your Family Through the Challenges of Unemployment

You're handling the e-wave as best you can, and you're steadily working your way toward reemployment. But you're aware that your job loss is also taking a toll on your spouse, children, and other family members. Are they struggling with the same emotions as you? If so, how much support can you expect from them? How can you help everyone face the difficult times ahead?

The Worst that Can Happen

Unemployment affects every aspect of, and person in, your life, including family members and close relations. When you're out of work, whatever issues already exist in your household tend to be magnified. At worst, unemployment can rock the foundations of weak families and bring everything down. In the same way as you'd glimpse the rocks and sediment at the bottom of a river if you drained away the water, you often see the troubled aspects of domestic relationships more clearly when unemployment hits. For example, if you've had problems communicating with family members in the past, unemployment aggravates this tendency and likely makes it even more difficult to talk openly. Similarly, if your mate, children, or other family members typically prey on your vulnerabilities, unemployment provides them with all sorts of juicy opportunities to exploit you. Family members may hurt you, inadvertently or not, with phrases like "Your friend is still employed, so what *really* happened to you?" "This only proves what I've known about you for some time." "You probably had it coming." "I can't imagine what the neighbors must be saying now." "You'll never get another job." "You've always been worthless…." and so on. If your marriage was tenuously held together, by money or by the prestige associated with your profession, your job loss may even dissolve the relationship once and for all.

You're in It Together

If you're privileged (as I was) to be surrounded by supportive family members, you have a "grounding force" while you're unemployed. Your spouse, children, and other close relatives can help you keep your problems in perspective by reminding you that life exists beyond the business world and ensuring that you don't have to face an uncertain future alone. In addition, your family can help provide the stability and continuity you crave while you're unemployed and while you make the transition from your old job to your new one. In return, you can help your spouse, children, and other relatives cope with the short-term changes they face while you're seeking reemployment.

In the following pages, I describe how unemployment is likely to affect your family members for better and for worse. You learn PIT-tested techniques for coping with the problems that unemployment commonly raises for families. And you discover how, if you have a solid domestic foundation, you can maximize your family's chances of emerging from the reemployment experience whole and ready to face whatever challenges and opportunities lie ahead together.

PIT TRICK: Create a partnership with your spouse and other family members to help pull each other through your unemployment.

The Family Wave

In the previous chapter, I described the e-wave (emotional wave) stages you're likely to experience while you're out of work: (1) shock and denial, (2) fear and panic, (3) anger, (4) bargaining, (5) depression, and (6) temporary acceptance. Now let's talk about the "f-wave," which is my shorthand term for the "family wave," or what your family members experience while you're unemployed. The f-wave parallels the e-wave in terms of its stages, but typically, it doesn't follow the same sequence or pace for them as the e-wave that's affecting you.

If the e-wave and f-wave were in sync, unemployment would be a bit easier for everyone. You could work through the grieving and healing process together, offering each other mutual support every step of the way. But that's generally not how it works. What elicits shock and disbelief for you may trigger your spouse's anger, and what brings you closer to temporary acceptance may catapult your kids into depression or fear. Your e-wave cycle may just be starting up again, perhaps because of a job rejection you received, while your family members are finally coming to grips with your unemployment and reaching the end of their f-wave cycles.

If your goal is to support your loved ones while you're unemployed, then you have to keep abreast of which f-wave stages they're experiencing at all times. That means making an effort to ask how everyone is feeling and what you can do to help, no matter what you're going through. Don't just assume that your family members' concerns and emotions are in sync with yours.

Similarly, keep in mind the special ways in which unemployment affects your children. Younger kids probably don't understand enough about your job loss to react in the same way as do adult members of your household. But that doesn't mean they are unscathed by your unemployment or that the f-wave doesn't affect them. On the contrary, your kids feel the anxiety and tension that pervades your home, and they hear adults whispering in worried tones. That may trigger surprisingly adult emotional reactions, such as panic and catastrophizing. As a result, your kids need your continuous love, reassurance, and guidance as much as the adults in your household who are fully in the know. So take the time to offer them an age-appropriate explanation of your job loss. Emphasize the fact that any consequences of your unemployment are short-lived and that, together, the family can handle any problems that arise.

PIT TRAP: Don't make the mistake of believing young children aren't affected by your unemployment.

As the World Turns Downward

When your family loses its sole or significant source of income, it can seem like the end of the world. Finances usually take center stage; expenses that never worried you before suddenly loom as ominous clouds. How will you pay the mortgage or keep up with your insurance and utility bills? Luxuries you could afford last week—dining out, vacations, summer camp, and similar enjoyments—necessarily grind to a halt.

In addition, your established role in the family may be threatened. If you were the infallible breadwinner and you temporarily cannot provide for your loved ones (at least in the manner to which they've been accustomed), members of your household can suffer a crisis of faith. For the same reasons, your self-esteem can take a nosedive, and you're likely to be overwhelmed with guilt. To make matters worse, if you're suddenly around the home most of the time when, historically, you were an unobtrusive or even invisible figure, you may find yourself in the way. You may even feel like a burden on your working spouse and a dead weight for your entire household to bear.

Regardless of the details, your family has to deal with a host of changes, and that poses challenges for everyone concerned. However, if you understand the issues that are likely to arise—particularly your family's feelings of powerlessness and the rising tensions in your household—and prepare yourself to handle them, you are well on your way toward successfully guiding your family through the reemployment process.

Powerlessness

Your spouse and children's immediate grief is, in many cases, less intense than yours. Unemployment creates ups and downs in their lives, just as it does in yours. But it's you, not your family, who has been cast out from the working world. Although your spouse, children, and other relatives can commiserate with you, they're grieving your job loss secondhand. They're experiencing sudden upheaval and uncertainty in their lives, but unlike you, they don't feel as though they've been personally violated.

Because they're on the periphery of your job loss, they may also feel a sense of helplessness. As you're the one who's unemployed, you're in control of the reemployment process, and you're able to call all the shots. Your family members can only watch from the sidelines as you make your own decisions and your own mistakes.

In addition, their lack of control over the reemployment process undoubtedly leaves them frustrated, frightened, and angry. To counter your family's feelings of powerlessness, you have to find ways to put them in the driver's seat as much as possible. Following are some approaches that have worked for PIT members:

■ **Make your spouse a total fiscal partner.** Look at the family's income and expenses together, and assess your financial picture realistically. Start by adjusting your budget. Decide with your spouse which luxuries, such as expensive vacations, you can postpone or temporarily eliminate. At the same time, determine the non-negotiables that you will maintain at all costs. When

I was out of work, for example, my wife and I determined that our daughter would go to camp no matter what—even though it meant no family vacation. The key for proactive budget analysis and planning is to include your significant other as a co-decision maker for all of the issues involved in the household's finances.

- **Set new priorities for your family's remaining income**, again making your spouse or other adults in the household full partners. When you've agreed on a plan, share it with your children and answer their questions about the immediate situation and the short-term future.

- **Assign measurable, money-saving tasks to family members.** For instance, older kids might wash the car or mow the lawn, and younger children might be responsible for clipping coupons or turning off lights in empty rooms. Let your children know how much their efforts contribute to the family's savings.

- **Solicit your family's help in creating no-cost, appealing substitutes** for the pleasures you can't afford. For example, Jack and his wife, who loved to eat at fancy restaurants once a week, found enjoyment instead in preparing low-cost, homemade gourmet meals. Your family might try playing cards or board games at home instead of supporting your local cinema conglomerate. That might make a monthly family outing more special—unless, of course, you decide it would be fun to eliminate them completely.

Rising Tensions

When your family is cycling through the f-wave and you're traversing the e-wave, minor irritations can erupt into significant conflicts. Any unresolved aspects of your relationships with your spouse, children, and other relatives rise to the surface. Even small nuisances, such as failing to take out the trash or leaving the dishes in the sink, can become focal points of ferocious battles.

Tension can reveal itself in other ways, too. You may begin to feel jealous of a spouse who goes off to work every day and leaves you behind to wallow in your misery. Your kids, too, can unintentionally hurt you by demanding sneakers you can't afford or throwing broken promises (such as canceled ski trips) in your face. But all the tension in your household doesn't originate with others; some of it begins with you.

Because your livelihood has been unceremoniously snatched a-way, you may be susceptible to a condition that PIT members have dubbed the "crazies," in which you exhibit erratic behavior, unpredictable emotional surges, and impulsive, inexplicable choices. (For example, a PIT member who'd been bemoaning his lack of money suddenly stunned his spouse by buying a brand-new, fire engine red, luxury convertible that the family didn't want or need.) In place of the predictable, responsible person your family members knew and trusted, there may be an unfathomable stranger sitting at the table dining with them each night. The crazies come and go according to which e-wave stage you're confronting, and no one is quite sure what mood to expect from you from one minute to the next.

Here are some suggestions to stem the negative effects of rising tension and the crazies in your household:

- Make sure everyone understands that unemployment is a temporary condition and not a disease. Emphasize that the tension and the crazies will also pass.
- Recognize and intervene when family members try to turn each other into scapegoats. Sometimes the solution is as simple as leaving the room when hostility surfaces.
- Find productive, victim-free ways to let off steam (see Chapter 2 for ideas about coping with anger).

PIT TRICKS: Immediately increase your level of daily exercise. You'll feel better both physically and emotionally; in addition, an exercise break can provide much-needed personal space and cool-down time.

What Else You Can Do

In addition to the tips for dealing with your family members' powerlessness and the rising tensions in your household, there are steps you should take to maintain a stable and positive domestic life while you're unemployed. These actions fall into three main categories: communicating, establishing a new role for yourself, and maintaining normality.

Communicate

Open and honest communication is a critical part of helping your family through the trauma of your job loss. PIT "pacesetters"—those who rebound from unemployment most quickly and successfully— typically make their spouses (and sometimes their children) partners in their reemployment efforts. These pacesetters gently tell family members that they've lost their jobs as soon as it happens so that the family doesn't learn about it from another source (such as a sympathetic former coworker who calls the house to make sure everyone is all right). Also, during their job search, pacesetters update their spouses and children as much as possible without alarming them.

Family members can pat you on the back, act as coaches and cheerleaders, and help you celebrate your accomplishments while you're out of work. However, they should never be licensed to grill or bully you. They won't help you by taking on the role of taskmasters. You can "hire" a buddy to ask how many letters you've sent out, when you plan to make follow-up phone calls, and the like. But don't assign the bad-guy role to your spouse or kids.

Encourage your family members to share their feelings with you, too. Your spouse, children, and other relatives may want to soften the blow of your unemployment by hiding their fears, frustrations, and disappointments. It's your job to get the truth out of them, with kindness and sensitivity. Don't let them suffer silently; do whatever it takes to keep the channels of communication open.

Establish a New Role for Yourself

While you're out of work, you need to redefine your responsibilities. This is especially important in what was a dual-income family; if your spouse is away all day, it might make sense for you to take on the domestic chores. PIT members often use their free time to cook dinner, get the dry cleaning, shop for groceries, pick up the kids from daycare, drive them to after-school events, and the like.

However, your reemployment efforts must come first, because *finding a new job is your full-time job*. Be sure that all family members are clear about their expectations and reassignments of household duties. Don't assume more than your fairly adjusted share of responsibilities out of misguided guilt or shame about the fact that you're unemployed; ultimately, that could sabotage your job search.

Maintain Normality

Unemployment affects virtually every aspect of your life: your daily routines, social interactions, steady income, community standing, and a host of other things you probably took for granted before the ax fell. Now those things have vaporized along with your career. In the face of all that, how can your family life go on as before?

It doesn't, of course. Expect practical changes in your household so as to accommodate your new financial realities. But you don't have to sacrifice your family's mental health or sense of security in the process if you work hard at protecting the normality of your life.

Don't make any major life decisions, such as moving to a less expensive house, selling your assets, and the like, until the dust has settled. A defeatist attitude doesn't solve your monetary problems; proactive efforts to preserve critical aspects of your family's life do. Let your lenders, creditors, and utility companies know as soon as possible that you've lost your job, and negotiate temporary payment plans with them. Stress your intention to pay your debts in full as soon as you can. You may run into stumbling blocks, but your persistence will likely pay off.

It did for me. In my case, I was able to get a forbearance agreement that entitled me to pay a fraction of my mortgage until I went back to work. But that happened only after a clerk had repeatedly deflected my request to arrange a temporary repayment plan, sternly warning me that if a payment was missed, the bank would foreclose on my property. Only after I wrote the bank's president a letter detailing my dilemma did I receive a call from an executive assistant who was willing (and empowered fortunately) to negotiate a payment arrangement.

Once you've taken control of the most important household matters, you can focus on quality-of-life issues. Your spouse, kids, and you will get cabin fever if you're so afraid to spend money that you never go anywhere. But with a bit of creativity, you can find inexpensive ways of getting out and doing things together. Check your local library for free museum passes (many museums also offer no-cost admission one day a week or month) or local tourist attractions, seek out restaurants that have kids-eat-free specials, and scout for affordable events, such as kids' concerts, plays, or puppet shows. Go for family drives to surprise destinations (a beach, friend or relative's home, conservation site, and so on). Focus on abundance, whenever you can, instead of scarcity.

You may not be able to take your spouse and children to see first-run movies, but you can still borrow videotapes from the library. I remember a Saturday while I was out of work when my family needed to get away from our problems. We were short on cash, so we packed a picnic lunch and went to a neighborhood park. My wife, daughter, son, and I enjoyed the scenery, munched our sandwiches, and took turns flying a kite that we'd never used before. It turned out to be one of the best days I can remember, and it didn't cost us a cent.

It's also important to keep the romance alive in your marriage while you're unemployed. One former PIT member recalls that she served a special dinner-for-two with a glass of wine by the fireplace once a week. This simple ritual gave their relationship the boost it needed—regardless of how the job search was progressing.

Finally, always remember the vital importance of keeping your reemployment actions separate from family life. You can't look for a job twenty-four hours a day, seven days a week, so make time to be a parent, spouse, and part of the family. When you're finished with the day's job hunting efforts, leave it behind so you can fully participate in whatever is on your family's agenda.

Payoffs of Unemployment

Job loss unquestionably drags families through intense emotional stress and discomfort. But believe it or not, it's also likely to provide hidden benefits. Many PIT members feel more secure about their future after they have lost a job and later enjoyed successful reemployment. As one professional put it: "The worst thing that could possibly happen to me—getting fired—did happen. And I lived through it. Now there's nothing left for me to fear about my professional life." Other PIT members find that unemployment provides them with an opportunity to rethink their priorities and reflect on what's most important to them. Their focus inevitably shifts away from fast cars and fancy shoes as they embrace a simpler way of life.

You don't hear much about the benefits of job loss when a manufacturer downsizes or a phone company lays off fifteen hundred workers. But, trite as it may sound, the payoffs are real. In fact, a PIT member recently told me that unemployment was "the best thing that ever happened" to him. When Jim lost his job, he and his wife withdrew their daughter from daycare to save money. He became his daughter's primary caretaker, and he was there to see her take her first steps. As he explained at a subsequent PIT meeting, "I spent 90 percent of my time on the road when I was working. If I'd been my usual high-powered self last week, I certainly wouldn't have seen my beautiful daughter learn how to walk. No one told me I'd actually find joy in unemployment, but there it is."

Your new sense of security and shift in priorities will likely linger long after you've accepted a new job. When I was out of work, for instance, I was able to spend more time than ever before with my family. Each morning I would take my older child to school, and some days I would surprise her by "popping in" to the cafeteria just before lunch time with her favorite meal. Unemployment also created opportunities to help Annie with her homework and just share quality time with all my family. My wife, Donna, stood by me throughout the eight months that it took me to find permanent reemployment. Times were tough, but our love and commitment grew stronger as we faced our difficulties together. That was a great time of bonding for all of us and, in some ways, I've missed it since being reemployed. I guess my kids have, too.

Several years ago, I got a call at work from my son, Johnny, who was then eight. He told me that he wished I could be with him, and I was deeply touched. Fortunately, I'd accrued some compensation time and was able to indulge my parental instincts; without hesitation, I dropped what I was doing and came home. Johnny opened the door, saw me, and the look on his face said he was the most delighted little boy in the world. We shared a hug, played a board game, and then Annie, Johnny, and I cooked dinner together. When Donna got home, we all enjoyed a leisurely meal. As much as I enjoyed the family time prompted by Johnny's spontaneous phone call, I know this never would have happened before I lost my job. True, in my last position, I had the luxury of coming and going as I pleased. But back then, I simply didn't understand the value of my wife and kids as well as I do now. Your job loss, too, can become the catalyst for far-reaching, positive changes in your life, and you can draw strength from your family members as you never have before.

Now that your family is on the road to coping with your job loss, you can begin the inner work you need to relaunch your career. The following chapter presents exercises to help you determine in which direction to take your career next, and to establish where you fit in the new world of work.

Begin the Bounce-Back Beguine

Reinventing the Professional You

After days or weeks of riding the e-wave, you've begun to come to terms with your job loss, and you're now ready to forge ahead and face the working world again.

But it's been years since you really thought about what you want to do for a living. Conclusions you drew back then about what you wanted to do with your professional life and what your capabilities were may not apply any longer. It might be time to change jobs, and perhaps industries, even if that means going back to school or relocating to a distant place with your family. Also, the landscape of the workplace seems to have undergone a complete transformation since the last time you were in the job market. Once-booming industries have now dried up or exported their jobs to other states or countries. Most help-wanted ads you come across include unfamiliar techno-babble. Kids just out of college, with their natural computer prowess, now seem better qualified than you for your old position, let alone a better-paying or more satisfying one.

How do you decide what you want to do with the rest of your career and where you fit into the new world of work? How can you examine your choices and decide the best path to take while you work through job-loss trauma? Fortunately, you probably have all the answers right in your head. You just need a little prompting to put them on the table.

What Should You Do?

You're free. You have no work commitments, no professional appointments that you absolutely must keep, and nobody to answer to except yourself. Sure, you have to go back to work so you can pay the bills, and you'll honor that responsibility. But unless you're seriously strapped for cash, you don't have to rush it. Before you search for a job just like the last one, why not pause and consider your options? After all, you didn't choose to be unemployed. But now that you are, you have a rare opportunity to take the time to assess, and possibly redirect, your career.

If you're like most people, you probably decided how you'd make a living based on what other people told you about your skills, your interests at the time (if you were lucky), your major in school, and the opportunities that came your way. Your decision may have been well grounded then, but that doesn't mean you should, or must, stick by it now. You've had enough job-related and life experiences so that your career decisions can be based on your personal talents and abilities rather than fate or guesswork.

There's no magic formula to learning from your job-related and life experiences—it all comes down to hard, introspective work that entails taking an honest look at yourself and asking key questions about your strengths, weaknesses, likes, and dislikes. At PIT, we tell new members that they must truly know themselves before they can begin an effective marketing campaign. Achieving reemployment requires you to match your abilities and personal skill sets to an employer's needs. You are better able to do this once you've done the necessary inner work and answered the key questions in this chapter.

There are many excellent books devoted to helping you learn

about your professional self and choose a new career direction (see Appendix B for some of my favorites), and qualified counselors who can provide you with batteries of tests and vocational advice (more information about career counselors in Chapter 5). However, the most critical step boils down to discovering what to do and where you want to do it. PIT members have used the following questions and exercises to hone in on these present-day realities. I believe you, too, can use the questions and exercises in this chapter to gather information about the person and the professional you've become and to decide whether you want to stay the course or change your career direction.

Ask yourself the questions in this chapter and work through the various exercises provided. Then jot down the insights they inspire. I'm not suggesting that you spend the next month or two toiling over ponderous writing assignments. But you do need to plan adequate strategic time to complete a personal inventory of your skills before you begin the journey on the road to gainful reemployment. When you put on paper the truths about your professional life, you can isolate the keywords—those that describe your skills, strengths, interests, and goals—and use them as the basis for your résumé and cover letters (see Chapter 6). You can also compare the keywords to the buzz terms in help-wanted ads and look for close matches. Moreover, you can look for patterns in your answers that suggest ways to find success and satisfaction in the workplace.

You can also add other thought-provoking questions and complete the in-depth exercises in the books listed in Appendix B. Some excellent exercises are contained in *What Color Is Your Parachute?* by Richard Nelson Bolles. Another series of exercises (including résumé and cover letter templates) developed in response to requests from PIT members are in the *Career Bounce-Back! Reemployment Toolbox* workbook, which is available at www.careerbounceback.com. Stick with the exploration process. The insights you gain may become the beacon that guides you safely to the next stage of your career.

Step 1: Figure Out Where You've Been

You take your first step toward your future by looking back at what you've done with your career. No experience you've ever had, regardless of how it ended, has been a waste of time. Everything you've done has taught you about yourself: what you're capable of doing, what you like, what you hate, and what you need. The jobs you've held are no exceptions. Now that you have a bit of distance from your last work experience, you can view your past job and prior positions from a new perspective. Here's a starter list of questions you can ask to reveal key information:

- What did I like best about my last job? What did I like least?
- What did I like best, and least, about the company?
- What did I like best, and least, about the people with whom I worked?
- What did I like best, and least, about the people for whom I worked?
- What were my most important and satisfying accomplishments?
- How else might I have contributed to the company?
- What skills, education, and training would I have needed to make these contributions?
- What were my most significant failures?
- What kind of positive feedback did I receive from others?
- What kind of negative feedback did I receive?
- What skills did I gain while I was employed in my last job?
- In what other ways did I grow as a professional?
- What was missing from my last job that I would seek in a new position?

Now ask yourself these same questions about other (including volunteer) positions that you've held. Knowing where you've been—and what you did, didn't do, and wish you'd done while you were there—is the first step toward building a new career in which you can achieve personal satisfaction and professional success.

Step 2: Compare Work Experiences

Now that you've journeyed back in time to remember the jobs that you've held, compare those jobs. Ask yourself:

- In which job(s) was I happiest, and why?
- In which job(s) was I most successful, and why?
- Who was the best boss I ever had, and why?
- Who was the worst boss I ever had, and why?
- What significant barriers have stunted my career growth?
- If I could start my career over again, what kinds of things would I do differently?

PIT TRICK: Take the time to assess where you've been before you decide your next step.

Step 3: Do a Quick Take

Over the years, many PIT members have confessed that they're not sure what they want to do. I have therefore begun routinely handing out packets of fill-in charts and questionnaires to those who are attending their first PIT meetings. My experience has shown that the following exercises are most useful in helping professionals identify their changing skills, needs, and goals.

- In story or essay form, write your ten greatest accomplishments and your ten greatest disasters. Be sure to be as detailed as possible. You can, at your discretion, use work-related and professional tales, or those that are not, or a combination of both. Look for the commonalities among your successes, and then find out what your failures share as well. This gives you some insight into your strengths and weaknesses.
- Write several versions of your own obituary. The first should be the notice that would appear if you died today. The second should be the obituary people will read in ten or twenty years

if you follow the most probable career path. The third should be the obituary you'd want if you could follow the career path of your choice. This eye-opening exercise can help you quickly put your career choices and your job search into perspective.

■ Ask three of your closest friends to evaluate your strengths and weaknesses. Invite them to offer their input on your career path. Friends can have helpful insights, but be warned: They can also be brutally honest as they offer you their no-holds-barred impressions.

■ Diagram your career path from its beginning to the present, noting the highs and lows. Note whether you've consistently moved ahead, stalled, or rolled backward in your quest for career satisfaction and success. Then ask yourself the critical question: Do you want to stay the course and see where the path you've traveled so far will lead? Or is it time to move into an as-yet-unexplored direction?

Step 4: Find the Professional You

It's easy to lose your confidence and your perspective when you've recently been terminated. But losing a job doesn't make you any less of a professional. It simply presents a challenge to be overcome. Take the opportunity now to assess yourself as a person and as an employee. These questions provide a starting point:

■ How would I describe myself as a manager?

■ How have I typically reacted to extreme stress and pressure?

■ What have been the most difficult kinds of work problems I've had to handle?

■ What are the best career decisions I've made, and why?

■ What are some words that best describe me as a person?

■ In what way(s) would I like to be different from how I am?

■ What aspects of my personality have been barriers to my effectiveness or success?

■ How do I typically react when I'm criticized?

- What makes me angry?
- What things in life are most important to me?
- How would I define success?
- Using my definition of success, do I consider myself successful? Why or why not?
- If I did not have to work, what would I be doing?
- What do I like and dislike about work in general?
- What are some of the rewards I expect from work?
- What are some of the benefits an employer would enjoy by having me on its team?
- What am I best trained to do next?
- What are my short-range and long-term career objectives?
- Have I, in the past, ruled out any career alternatives that I would now like to reconsider?
- What career alternatives appear to be most logical at this point?
- What other alternatives do I have?

Step 5: Dream a Dream

If you're like most people, you've been living for more than just work during the last years. Many times the things that you most enjoyed doing and received the greatest level of gratification from weren't work related. Don't trivialize your hobbies and interests; what they've taught you and what you value about them are important considerations now, too, as you prepare to step back into the workplace. Look for transferable skills that you've acquired in your leisure time. Perhaps you've conducted research, tutored, written, coached, collected, analyzed, programmed, or managed. The knowledge you've gained, and the skills you've employed, might qualify you to pursue an alternative career or advance further in your old one.

Even though you're paid for doing your job, you can still enjoy it. People use their talents and abilities to start their own successful businesses, paint saleable pictures, write publishable novels, and import marketable goods from around the globe all the time. They make a living doing what they most want to do, and they're no better, smarter, or luckier than you—they've simply chosen to live their dreams. They made the commitment to "do what you love" (as Marsha Sinetar put it), and the money followed. Of course, it's always safer to experiment when you have a steady paycheck coming in. When you can count on an employer to cut you a check regularly, you feel more comfortable taking risks and launching your dream venture outside of working hours.

On the other hand, when you're locked into a job, you have less incentive and energy to explore alternative career possibilities. You become enmeshed in the demands of your job and the expectations of your company. But now that you're between careers, you have an opportunity to do what you've always wanted to do, at least to the extent that you have a cushion of safety in the form of severance pay and unemployment compensation. So what do you have to lose by testing the waters?

Indulge in a flight of fancy. If you could turn your hobbies and interests into a money-making venture for yourself, would you? Close your eyes for a few minutes and see yourself engaged in your dream job. (Alternatively, you might imagine yourself doing what you like best, or something you've done in the past that's given you incredible satisfaction.) Visualize, down to the smallest details, your environment, the people and objects around you, and what you're doing. Use all your senses. Hear the sounds, feel the textures, smell the aromas, and taste the tastes. Imagine that it's happening now, and take the time to experience it fully. Then open your eyes, and—keeping hold of the image—consider the following:

- What are the most appealing aspects of my fantasy?
- What are the most realistic aspects?
- What are the most absurd?
- What goals would I have to achieve to make my fantasy come true?
- What are the barriers to achieving those goals?
- How can I overcome them?

PIT TRICK: Break out of the professional "box" you've put yourself into, and consider all the things you'd really like to do as viable career moves.

Where Should You Do It?

In steps 1 through 5 of the previous section, you've analyzed your work history, characterized yourself as a professional, and examined your dreams to learn more about who you are and what you'd like to do. Now it's time to put it all together. In this section, you'll assess your career goals and desires, determine how feasible they are, and if necessary, temper your previous insights with reality.

For example, while comparing your work experiences in step 2 you may have determined that your best shot at personal happiness and career satisfaction lies in becoming a total quality management facilitator at a widget manufacturing plant. However, if the world's population has bought enough widgets to last forever and all the widget manufacturing companies are closing their doors, you need to know that so you can switch gears or transfer your skills. Or if an up-and-coming company in a promising new industry will have the best-paying quality-control positions for the foreseeable future, you should know about that, too—it just might cause you to redirect your job-hunting energies. This section provides a starter list of questions and exercises to help you assess the changing workplace and how you best fit into it.

Step 6: Survey the Field

Even if you've been working in the same industry throughout your career, that doesn't mean you have to stay in it for the duration. Before you commit yourself to a job search that once again targets that industry, do your homework. You're in the experimental mode, so you can be more flexible than you were in the past about what to do next. Depending on what you do for a living, it might be a relatively simple matter to transfer many of your skills and interests from one industry to another. For example, if you've been employed as a research scientist at a university for the past ten years, you might find it easy to cross over into the biotechnology industry. (In fact, as most experts predict that the biotechnology field will grow in the years ahead, such a career move could be wise.) Or you might use your math educator's background to enter the textbook publishing field. Even if you've received specialized training that you can't immediately envision using in another industry, there's no reason to feel stuck or pursue a future in a field that no longer interests you. It's hard enough to be successful searching for a job you believe you'd enjoy; you certainly don't need to stack the odds against yourself by half-heartedly chasing a position you've come to dislike. With additional training, you might be able to begin a career that makes sense for you now and in the context of today's workplace. Keep an open mind about what kind of business you want to approach next. Ultimately, you do a reality check on your field survey and career direction when you begin your informational interviewing (see Chapter 7); for now, though, continue with your field survey by reading trade magazines, industry newsletters, and local and national business newspapers. Attend trade shows and association meetings. Assess the current state of your industry and the changes that are in store for it. Begin with the following questions:

- How do industry experts rate the field's health today?
- What major changes are being predicted for the field?
- What factors will help the industry during the next decade?
- What are the biggest threats to the industry in the next decade?
- In what geographical areas will the field be the strongest?
- What types of people and skills will be in the greatest demand?
- Which jobs will be the best paying?
- Which jobs will be phased out?
- What advantages and disadvantages to working in the field currently loom largest?

Alternative career questions may also include:

- With my current skills, is the field still a good match for me?
- Are there additional classes I must take to achieve longevity in the industry, and how would I feel about taking them?
- Over the long haul, would the industry be able to compensate me enough to meet my financial needs?
- Would I be able to stay close to home for the foreseeable future if I stayed in my field?
- If not, would my family and I be willing to relocate to the geographical areas where the industry is growing?

Be sure to consider your needs and preferences, and those of your family members. Are there other industries to which you could transfer your job skills and interests? Would any of these be a better match for you? Put other industries that show potential through the same rigorous examination as your own. Arm yourself with all the information needed to decide if a change of direction makes sense for you.

PIT TRAP: Don't dismiss the idea of transferring your skills to new, emerging industries just because you haven't yet had professional experience in them.

Step 7: Writing Out a Plan

Structuring your thoughts by using charts can be an important part of the process of reentering the workplace and considering career changes. Writing out a career plan creates personal direction and focus. A written career plan is a tangible and measurable outcome of the self-commitment needed to reinvent the professional you.

Exploring Alternatives

In this part of the chapter, I offer you some charts that have helped PIT members work through their industry- and job-related questions. Try to find some quiet time and space so that you can carefully consider your answers, and fill in these charts.

Now that you've given some thought to your career plans and conducted some research into the economic realities, write down ten job options on the worksheet below.

Ranking Career Alternatives

❒ _____

❒ _____

❒ _____

❒ _____

❒ _____

❒ _____

❒ _____

❒ _____

❒ _____

❒ _____

Next, you need to describe the positives and negatives for the options you uncovered in the previous exercise. For each option, use the following form. Add additional sheets if you need more space.

Evaluating Your Options

Option _____

Pros _____

_____

_____

Cons _____

_____

_____

Once you finish evaluating your choices, jot down the hurdles to turning each option into a reality. Create a time line by assigning each step an action date. Again, use additional space if necessary.

Option _____

Hurdles	Action Steps	Action Dates
_____	_____	_____
_____	_____	_____
_____	_____	_____
_____	_____	_____
_____	_____	_____
_____	_____	_____

Step 8: Create a Personal Mission Statement and Career Summary

Congratulations! You've taken the eight critical steps toward assessing your work and life experience and deducing where you would best fit into the workplace. Now it's time to boil down what you've learned into a personal mission statement. The answers to the questions of what you want to do with the rest of your career, and where you ought to do it, didn't come to you without thought. You had to do your homework and engage in much soul searching to find your direction. On the other hand, now that you've identified what you want from your career and where you're likely to find it, you can capture it on paper as a first step to reentering the workplace. Write a few sentences that describe who you are and where you're going. The result is your mission statement. Personal mission statements have helped PIT members focus their job searches and sell themselves to employers. You can also transform an abbreviated mission statement into the career summary on your résumé.

Your mission statement sets forth your current goals. These may change during the course of your job search and beyond. For that reason, you'll want to reevaluate your mission statement once a year. Each time you update your mission statement, you should project five years into the future, even though you may well change it in the interim to keep pace with your personal and career growth. Your five-year mission statement provides you with a long-range plan and reminds you of your shorter-term goals. It serves as your road map and your beacon, so don't be shy about framing yours and hanging it in a prominent place where you can see it every day.

PIT TRICK: Create an ambitious mission statement for yourself because you'll soar only as high as you dare.

Putting Your Job Plan into Action

You now have a strategic road map detailing where you want to go and the industry in which you want to work. This is half the battle to achieving success. The rest entails developing a personal "infra-structure" that helps you carry out an effective job search. The infra-structure that's worked for PIT members includes four key elements.

Establish a Daily Routine

Unemployment isn't a vacation. It is now your full-time job to find a full-time job. To do that, you have to stay sharp. The world goes on according to its usual schedule, and you have to match it by creating—and sticking to—your own routine. Even though you no longer have to follow a schedule to please your boss, you still need to set fixed times to get up, complete your job search-related tasks, knock off for the day, and eat. This keeps you in sync with prospective employers and keeps cobwebs and brain rust from forming. It also reinforces your daily commitment to finding reemployment.

PIT TRICK: Stay in sync with the working world by es-tablishing a daily routine and sticking to it.

Develop a Winning Attitude

To move effectively through the reemployment process, you must be proactive and positive. Today's working environment demands a strong sense of urgency, follow-through, and ability to anticipate and respond to employers' needs. It's your task to mobilize and put your plan into action. In the beginning, it may be difficult, and each day may be a struggle. But you have a responsibility to your family and yourself to maintain an attitude that helps you further your goals and move you through the reemployment process more quickly.

To a large extent, your personal attitude determines the ultimate success of your job campaign. If you're angry at your former employer or have a negative attitude for other reasons, it shows. Your personal attitude is the foundation upon which the road to reemployment is built. Attitude sets the stage for success and is apparent in your voice, posture, and presence. Hostility or negativity can keep your job search in limbo; a positive attitude can propel you over the finish line.

Create an Efficient "Office" Space

If you were able to negotiate with your former employer for the use of your old office and the company's equipment, great. Another terrific option is to barter with a small company or new business incubator in your area for office space—for example, you might provide computer consulting in exchange for the use of a desk, phone line, photocopier, and fax machine. Otherwise, you have to put some effort into turning a part of your home into a workplace. A separate room that's free from traffic is your best bet. However, if that isn't available, get creative. Use a book shelf, desk, or other large piece of furniture to definitively divide a room, and appropriate the quieter half. Ask family members to respect your working hours and to keep their voices down during that time.

Once you have an official, quiet "office," equip yourself with the materials you need to look and feel like a professional. Ideally, you'll have a separate phone line (or at least one that younger kids won't pick up when you're not home), an answering machine, and letterhead. A computer and printer are also critical job-search tools; if you don't own them, consider a rental or a walk-in service that allows you to use computer gear on-site by the hour. Or work out a deal to borrow a neighbor or friend's computer; you might be able to use it when no one else needs the online time in exchange for babysitting or house-sitting services, or the like.

You'll be in your office for long stretches of time, so keep yourself as comfortable as possible. Make sure there's adequate lighting. Take breaks for stretching and fresh air as frequently as you need them to keep yourself productive while you're in your job-search "headquarters." In addition, many PIT members (especially those with young children at home during the day) regularly use the library as an additional source for quiet space. Libraries contain reams of helpful, job-related information. Many also have computers with Internet access.

Track Results

Employment gurus estimate you'll hear "no" ninety-nine times from prospective employers before getting one "yes." Every time you get a rejection letter or someone slams a phone when you call, you should be thinking: "Great, I'm on rejection number 51. That means I only have 48 to go."

Whenever you contact someone, keep track of the person's name, title, and company; the date; your action; and the result. This paper trail is especially critical once you begin your rounds of informational interviews because you may well have to identify people quickly when they return your call, and the worst thing you can do is make them feel they're part of an undifferentiated cold-call or mass-mail campaign. You'll also be able to see, at a glance, the progress you've made.

As you follow these four steps, you lay the foundation for a successful job search and assume and maintain responsibility for your reemployment. Your next task is to assess the available job-hunting resources and decide which are most likely to help guide you through the following steps of your career planning.

CHAPTER 5

How to Find
Good Help Nowadays

Using Low-Cost/No-Cost
Job Hunting Resources

You have learned the critical lesson that comes with unemployment: Finding a job is your responsibility. No matter how much you "deserve" another chance in the workplace, the right job opportunity isn't just going to fall into your lap, nor will someone hand it to you on a silver platter. If reemployment is your goal, you have to make it happen for yourself.

Unfortunately, you're probably rusty in the job-hunting arena, if not new to it. You begin to think about headhunters and others out there who can help you. You might also think about taking advantage of some of the latest, high-tech job-hunting resources such as electronic classified ads and Web sites that post job listings. Surely, some of these people and re-sources would be valuable to you if you understood them and knew how to use them. But how do you avoid the time-consuming dead ends, the people of dubious competence or motives, and the innumerable job-hunting services that charge a lot but offer little value?

Rebuilding Your Network

By and large, professionals attending their first PIT meetings share one characteristic: They feel entirely alone in their job searches. In their previous positions, most of them had coworkers, assistants, or even a full complement of staff members who could help them handle hundreds of important and mundane tasks each week. Now, suddenly, they're on their own in a competitive, changing workplace. They haven't conducted a job search for years, and they don't know about the many tools and techniques that are available for job seekers. They're especially demoralized since their former coworkers and associates have stopped calling. In short, they feel entirely cut off from the workplace and from everyone in it who might help them.

I always encourage PIT members to take responsibility for their reemployment and to see their job search as a proactive process. They're the only ones who can steer their careers in the best possible direction and find a new position that's right for them. I explain that no one cares about their futures as much as they do and that, ultimately, their careers are in their own hands. At the same time, PIT members don't have to go it alone. However disconnected they may feel from the workplace, they can begin to reconnect with people. They can mobilize a network of "movers and shakers" and find resources that can jump-start their job search, increase their chances of successful placement, and provide moral support along the way.

In this chapter, I describe some of the human resources professionals and resources that are available. I'll talk about the two categories of HR help—traditional and high tech—and discuss ways to maximize the possible payoffs of each while avoiding their potential hazards. You won't find a single resource in this chapter that's guaranteed to hold the key to your successful future. But you will find trusted resources that have worked for PIT members and other job seekers who have used them judiciously while retaining control of their futures. And while you're evaluating the HR professionals and resources that are available, you're taking the first steps toward rebuilding your professional network and ultimately reentering the workforce.

Recruitment Firms

During the course of their careers, many PIT members were courted by recruiters with tantalizing offers of higher pay and tremendous opportunities for advancement. Based on that experience from when they were employed, recently unemployed PIT members often believe that there's a recruiter out there whose file cabinets are just brimming with jobs—all with their names on them. I've seen versions of this fantasy play itself out many times. In some cases, it actually happens, which is why you should contact recruiters as part of your job-search efforts. Professionals who know what they want to do with the next phase of their careers and are ready to enthusiastically pursue their goals may find recruiters who can help them. In fact, some of the most successful employee/recruiter relationships I've heard about have lasted beyond the actual job hunts and evolved over the years. A recruiter who believes in your value to the workplace can keep your name in front of potential employers in good and bad times alike. For these reasons, I recommend connecting with a number of recruitment firms, narrowing the possibilities down to one or two, and building a lasting relationship with one recruiter as a part of your job-search effort.

Choosing a Recruiter

Many of us tend to group all recruitment firms together, but these companies actually fall into two categories: those that charge employers for filling job openings, and those that charge job seekers a fee. Because money is a concern for most of the out-of-work professionals I encounter, I strongly favor the former type of recruitment firm. Even if you do have the time and money to hire an employee-paid recruiter, I don't recommend that option. In my experience, many of the recruiters who expect you to pick up the tab seem to be in business for the sole purpose of taking advantage of the unemployed. Certainly, not all employee-paid recruiters are charlatans. But I believe you have too many good uses for your time, energy, and dollars to sift through the employee-paid agencies and find those that may be exceptions to the rule.

Fortunately, you can choose from many hundreds of employer-paid agencies, some of which work with a broad band of positions and some of which deal with only specific industries and jobs. I always recommend working with specialized recruiters because they're apt to have better contacts in, and greater knowledge of, your industry. Therefore, they're more likely to match you up with a job in your field and provide useful career guidance along the way. Remember, even though there are many reliable, specialty-oriented headhunters to help you in your job search, you won't get the opportunity to interview unless you have an exact "ability match" with a specific job request for which they're recruiting. As recruiters fill open positions, they receive new job requests. That's why, once you find a recruiter, it's important to stay in touch throughout the job-search process. But don't wait for a recruiter to call you.

Of Cold Calls and Cold Shoulders

In a workplace paradox (similar to that in which help-wanted ads seek "experienced" entry-level workers), most recruiters prefer to work with professionals who are already employed. A headhunter's livelihood depends on orchestrating good job matches and preserving lucrative relationships with employers. In fact, *headhunters* is a misnomer; these professionals aren't in the business of hunting heads to fill jobs. Rather, their mission is to fill job openings with those candidates who are perceived by employers as the most qualified. They lay their reputations on the line every time they set up an interview with a potential employee, so they take care to work with only job candidates who, they're convinced, can solve an employer's problems. Unfairly or not, some recruiters may perceive unemployed people to be higher "risks" than those who already have jobs. Consequently, they're more likely to spend their time placing working professionals for job openings and may appear to have a bias against the unemployed. I've heard of PIT members who have mailed or faxed résumés to every specialty agency in the country they can find that focuses on their field without connecting with a single qualified recruiter who would help them.

The Networking Solution

Does this mean that you shouldn't bother with recruitment firms? No. But you should consider them just one of many reemployment resources. Also, think about how you approach recruiters. As I've just suggested, the shotgun approach is usually a waste of time and money and often leads to dashed hopes. Professionals In Transition who have successfully used recruiters to ease them back into the workplace took the time to network their way into the firms with which they wanted to be affiliated. Here's how, with persistence and common sense, you might duplicate their efforts.

- Your impressive, unsolicited, over-the-transom résumé or cold call usually won't garner much interest unless you can make a personal connection with a recruiter. The tried-and-true method of name dropping, on the other hand, is likely to serve you well. Ask successful professionals to provide introductions to recruiters with whom they have worked.
- You can also get referrals from people you speak with during informational interviews. It's far more effective to tell a recruiter in your cover letter, or during a phone conversation, "Jackie Smith, the civil engineer whom you placed a few years ago at the XYZ company, recommended I give you a call," than it is to send a blind résumé.
- If you've ever been contacted by a recruiter, and you still have the contact information, then begin by contacting that person. Also, ask friends in your profession to share your name with recruiters who cold call them. (Once you're employed again, you'll want to keep a file on all the recruiters who call you, and to whom you've referred qualified candidates. As I said earlier, you never know when you or someone you know will need a connection to a recruiter.)

■ You can also engage in "backwards networking" as a last resort. That means finding several recruitment firms that interest you in a phone book or classified section in the newspaper. Then check with everyone you know until you find a connection to the firms.

■ Once a recruiter does take the time to call you, it's time to sell him or her on yourself. Be upbeat and honest about your qualifications, as you would during a job interview. Make it clear that you're eager and able to move ahead with the next phase of your career.

PIT TRAP: Don't waste your time trying to sell yourself to an unwilling recruiter.

Do Your Homework

If you do network your way into a recruiter's firm that you've heard positive things about, you'll want to check further its credentials—especially if you're choosing between a number of recruiters. The most experienced and knowledgeable recruiters are designated by the National Association of Personnel Consultants as CPCs. In addition, the firm is probably a member of a professional organization or trade group. Here are some specific questions you can ask to help narrow your choices:

■ What's your "hit" rate with placing people in jobs similar to the one I'm seeking?

■ With which companies do you typically work?

■ What levels of workers do you regularly place, and at what salaries?

■ Are my qualifications similar to those of professionals whom you've successfully placed?

■ How long have you been in the recruitment business?

■ How old is your company?

Finally, ask for references—preferably, people who have been clients for years—and follow up. When all else is equal, stick with the recruiter with whom you feel most comfortable on a personal level. You want to work with an employment agent who can enthusiastically, and successfully, broker your skills and talents. Remember, you're not looking for a recruiter who will feel sorry for you or reluctantly represent you; there's a clear difference between selling yourself to a recruiter and twisting his or her arm to take you on. You don't want to waste an employment agent's time, nor do you want the agent to squander yours, if the partnership isn't right from the outset. A solid relationship with a recruiter begins with a good rapport between two professionals. Don't settle for less.

Before discussing the next resource category, career counselors, I want to touch upon the problem of having multiple recruiters work for you. If your work experience is impressive enough and your contacts are especially solid, or you're seeking a job in an industry that's experiencing a shortage of qualified professionals, you may have the luxury of finding more than one recruiter who expresses an interest in working with you. Then it's time to begin the selection process. It's perfectly acceptable to team up with more than one recruiter at a time, provided all parties know about each other. However, I have heard of instances where two recruiters presented your credentials to the same company. In such a scenario, it's likely that both recruiters would simply withdraw your candidacy to eliminate the hassle and protect their reputations—leaving you high and dry.

Even if you have the top recruiters in the world falling over you with offers of representation, a professional recruitment firm may not be the best resource for you at the moment. This is typically the case when you're undecided about which course your career should take; no recruiter can match you with a job if you don't know what type of job you're really seeking. In that case, it's probably time for some career counseling.

Career Counseling

You've already discovered that a recruiter can help you only if you know precisely the kind of job you're looking for, and if you can convince him or her that you're ready to wholeheartedly pursue it. However, if you're not yet a candidate for a recruiter's services, there's always another possibility: career counseling.

Finding the Right Career Counseling

It's critical to find the right kind of career counseling for your situation. There are client-paid (where you're the client and the payer of the bill) companies that specialize in career counseling, and there are also other sources of low-cost or no-cost career counseling. First I'll discuss the former: private, one-on-one career counseling.

A career counselor can help you with your job search in various ways, depending on the services offered. But you still hold the reins of your job search. A career counselor can be a great asset in your reemployment effort, but he or she can't do the work for you. Understand that you must play an active role in your career counseling sessions, beginning with hiring the right professional to help you. Just as you wouldn't look through the phone book to choose a psychotherapist, you shouldn't scan the Yellow Pages for a career counselor and engage him or her on the basis of a quick phone call with the receptionist. Ask other professionals who have received career counseling for recommendations. Personally interview those whose names come up most often, and narrow your prospects down to the two or three with whom you have the best rapport. Then compare their services, and figure out which gives you the most value for your money. Before you sign on the dotted line of a career counselor's contract, be sure you understand:

> ▦ **Exactly what services you're paying for.** Although career counselors all have the same job title, they may provide any combination of offerings, ranging from vocational testing and stress

management to résumé-writing help and interview coaching. You should never pay for more job-searching assistance than you need.

■ **How long the counseling process takes.** Find out the frequency of the sessions, and be sure you can reasonably incorporate them into your schedule.

■ **When the relationship ends.** Do you part company automatically when you find employment, or is continuing assistance available to you after that time at no extra charge?

■ **What if the counseling doesn't result in reemployment.** Ask whether you can come back at no charge if you find yourself out of work again. If so, what's the time period covered by the "guarantee"?

Of course, any career counselor whom you consider hiring should provide references. During your conversations with former and current clients, find out what benefits they have received from the career counseling. Remember that, as a consumer, you have a right and a responsibility to protect your investment of time, energy, and dollars.

Low-Cost or No-Cost Alternatives

If you can't afford the services of a private career counselor, or you want to "cherry-pick" among the career-counseling offerings available without burdening yourself financially, you'll be glad to know it's relatively easy to locate low-cost or no-cost services that can help you. Start by looking in the calendar section of your local newspaper to find out which career services are offered in your community. Many local libraries, colleges, churches, synagogues, and public employment agencies (whose fees are paid by your state, as contrasted with the employee- and employer-paid recruitment firms discussed earlier) offer job-hunting services to anyone who's out of work. These range from seminars that focus on résumé writing to workshops that help you hone your interviewing techniques. Attending these meetings gives you access to a wide range of professionals who will happily share a wealth of job-hunting advice with you.

Knowing who these information presenters are and understanding their hidden agendas gives you a better idea of what to expect from them. Perhaps a professional career counselor wants to add you to his or her client base, or a writer wants to pitch an expensive résumé makeover. That doesn't mean the presentation won't be worthwhile, but you should know if someone's hidden agenda is to sell you something so you can assess the advice accordingly.

Every job-hunting session you attend also provides an opportunity to network with other job seekers. Remember, just because someone is unemployed, or just because you met an individual at a local community college's free interviewing workshop, doesn't mean that person isn't a worthwhile contact for you. At PIT meetings, members who are out of work help each other make connections to potential employers all the time. That's one of the ways in which PIT works best, and you might get similar results by networking at job-hunting forums in your community.

Also, don't be shy about asking the local librarian or community college instructor for help with your job search. True, they are not professional career counselors. But they can steer you toward free vocational testing, books, or computers and other office equipment that's available to you while you're conducting your job search. It's part of their job, and you can find many experienced professionals who are glad of the opportunity to put their skills to use while helping you advance your marketing campaign.

Job Hunting High-Tech Style

In addition to walking the traditional avenues for locating a new job, you might want to consider cruising the information highway for an additional boost. The World Wide Web is teeming with sites for job hunters. All you need is an Internet connection, and you'll find a wealth of online job-search assistance. The challenge is figuring out where to begin and evaluating the many online services offered.

You might begin at PIT's Web site, www.jobsearching.org. From there I recommend www.careerbounceback.com, and then Richard Nelson Bolles' www.jobhuntersbible.com. This well-organized site provides links to places where you can find job listings, post your résumé, obtain career counseling and other job-hunting help, make contact with other professionals, and conduct research. It also offers advice for making the best use of the Web in your job search.

Alternatively, you can round up your own electronic job-hunting resources by using a popular search engine such as:

- AltaVista (www.altavista.digital.com)
- Yahoo (www.yahoo.com)
- Lycos (www.lycos.com)
- Hotbot (www.hotbot.com)
- Excite (www.excite.com)

A search on the terms *job* or *career* reveals thousands of related sites. Or you can use a subscriber-only service to hook into proprietary job-hunting resources. For example, America Online's Career Guidance Services includes "Federal Government Employment Opportunities," "Military Career Transition," "Working With Disabilities," and similar information.

Whatever approach you take to online job searching, you now have a good excuse to "surf the net." Potential employers are likely to be impressed with your electronic prowess, provided you demonstrate your ability to use the information you glean appropriately, creatively, and judiciously.

Track Your Online Hours

It's easy to get hooked on all the benefits the Internet offers job seekers. You can use the Web before your newspaper is delivered, on days when the local library and post office are closed, and after business hours to keep your job search moving. But if you're spending a disproportionate amount of your time in cyberspace, you may need to cut back on your electronic explorations.

Although the World Wide Web is a treasure trove of job-hunting resources, it can also be a time sink. Many of its offerings are passive, rather than active. For example, you may find thousands of job openings on the Web, but answering each one would be the equivalent of sending a response to every classified ad you see in newspapers around the country. This might feel productive and emotionally satisfying, but your success rate probably won't merit the expenditure of time and energy. You're no more likely to find the right job through electronic classified ads than you are via the conventional type. Many ads are outdated even before they hit your PC because they've already been filled; other advertised "vacancies" are merely database-builders for companies, and the jobs don't really exist. Even if an electronic ad is current and legitimate, you still need to read the fine print of electronic job listings. Carefully check the salaries, locations, responsibilities, and other details of any jobs that interest you before you respond to save yourself the disappointment, time, and embarrassment of chasing dead ends or inappropriate job leads. The quality of information available on the Web covers a wide spectrum. Some of it's worthwhile, some is outdated or dead wrong, and some falls in the middle. Therefore, you have to use discretion if you're getting something for nothing on the Web, just as you would in every other area of your job search.

PIT TRAP: Allocate your online time efficiently; don't waste endless hours in potentially low-return activities.

Electronic Networking

While the Web may be today's sexy job-hunting resource—and it's certainly worth exploring—no cyberspace site administrator is more likely than a recruiter or a career counselor to hand you a job. Just because you've posted your résumé to five hundred job databases and uploaded it to two hundred newsgroups, you can't expect the perfect position to leap out of your PC. If you want to make the best use of the Web's considerable job-hunting capabilities, you have to do just what you do in the offline world: network.

To make connections with professionals on the Web, you have to actively seek the professionals where they congregate. Newsgroups and listservs (electronic mailing lists) are great starting points. Once you've subscribed (there's no fee), you'll be able to exchange messages with group members. Take time to actively participate in electronic discussions so that members get to know you as an individual. Once you've contributed your ideas, mention to like-minded contributors that you're seeking a job in the industry. You're likely to acquire tips and information about companies that might hire people with a background similar to yours, and you can count on spreading the word that you're available and have much to contribute to the industry.

If you're looking for an entrée to specific professionals, you can use online directories such as Four11 (www. four11.com) or Switchboard (www.switchboard.com) to find their e-mail addresses. These are electronic phone books that contain telephone numbers, mailing addresses, and e-mail addresses. Use e-mail addresses as judiciously as you would phone numbers and snail-mail addresses; don't e-mail people unless you have a connection to them, if you can help it. If you must send an unsolicited e-mail message to a stranger, make your pitch concise and to the point (so as not to be confused with a "spammer"—that is, someone who regularly floods private e-mail boxes with unwanted, commercial junk mail), and be realistic about the results. A better, more effective alternative to sending "cold" e-mail messages is to send "warm" ones. Use the Web's people-finding resources creatively to connect with a potential employer or with someone who has access to him or her. For example, your college's online alumni directory or an association's electronic membership list might provide a starting point. An e-mail that says, "I'm Jane Donovan, a fellow alumna of Boston University class of 1972, and I'd like to know if you or anyone you know has worked with the financial departments of any hospitals in New England" will provide far better results than an e-mail that says, "You don't know me, but since you're a CFO at Massachusetts General, I thought you might be willing to talk to me about finance jobs that are available in New England-area hospitals."

Other Electronic Tools

In addition to the free job-hunting resources available on the Web, there are also electronic tools that you can buy via mail order, software companies, or local computer or software stores that can help you create résumés, assess your career strengths, and so on. I talk about these in the next chapter. In addition, I discuss new ways of using résumés and cover letters to reach people, and talk about how low-tech tools—the telephone and fax—can play an integral part in your job search.

Campaign for Success

Using Résumés and Cover Letters to Market Yourself Effectively

You know that you would be an asset to anyone who hired you. Now you just have to convince a potential employer of that fundamental truth. Unfortunately, the professionals you're about to contact are so over-loaded with information—including some from competing job seekers—that they can't begin to keep up with it all. This info glut creates two specific challenges. First, you must be sure that your pitch survives the "thirty-second countdown" that consigns most job-hunting communications to the circular file (also called "data heaven"). Second, to stand out, your pitch must elicit an especially favorable response from a potential employer. In short, you must compose concise and appealing written pitches that rise to the new challenges of the electronic age.

Making Every Second Count

At this point in the career bounce-back process, you've probably established a network of resources to help you with your job search. But the real work of finding a job still rests with you, and it lies ahead: It's your responsibility to market yourself directly to potential employers. Until you finally accept a job offer, that's how you're most likely to spend the majority of your workday.

You're already familiar with the marketing tools—the résumé and the cover letter—that you rely on during your job search. But if you haven't been in the job market for a while, you might not be aware of how today's technology can both help and hinder your efforts. Although computers and fax machines enable you to communicate with employers more easily than ever before, they make it almost too easy to apply for a job. Anyone with a couple of hours to spare can send hundreds of résumés and cover letters all over the world as part of a snail-mail or computerized mass-mailing campaign. Employers, therefore, are continuously besieged by résumés and cover letters. If they want to consider all or most of them, they have to move through the sky-high stack at a breakneck pace. What does that mean for you? In effect, you have about thirty seconds to impress a potential employer with your pitch—and the onus is on you to make every one of those seconds count.

In this chapter, I discuss how you can create résumés and cover letters that have the greatest chance of surviving the screening process and eliciting favorable responses. I also point out how you can tailor your pitches to meet the demands of the electronic age.

Putting Résumés and Cover Letters into Perspective

The first order of business for many job hunters is to revise their résumés and cover letters so they can begin their marketing campaigns. They believe it's possible to create the perfect résumé and cover letter, and they're determined to do so before they move ahead with their job searches. Unfortunately, there isn't any such thing as a résumé or cover letter that will please every employer, all of the time. No matter how much time and effort you put into them, written pitches remain works-in-progress. You can always find some way to improve them. However, when you agonize over your résumé and cover letter for longer than a week or so, you hold up your job search unnecessarily.

The sooner you feel satisfied enough with your written pitch to begin your marketing campaign, the better.

Besides, you reach a point of diminishing returns since, as I mentioned earlier, your résumé and cover letter will get only thirty seconds or so of an employer's time anyway. I once worked for a vice-president of marketing who explained how he managed all the résumés and cover letters that he received. He'd bring home five hundred sets of them and sort through the stack while he watched the Sunday night football game. With one eye on the television set, he'd single out ten "possibles" that might be worth following up at some point. He'd then dispatch the other 490 to a "recycle" pile that would land on his administrative assistant's desk on Monday morning. The administrative assistant would send out form letters assuring all the job seekers that their résumés were "currently being considered" and that they'd be notified when a suitable job opening became available. Once the administrative assistant had responded to all 490 résumés and cover letters, she'd bury them in the back of a storage room with thousands of others. None would ever see the light of day again.

At first glance, the vice-president's screening method might seem brutal. But if he hadn't streamlined the process of evaluating the five hundred-plus résumés and cover letters he received each week, he wouldn't have any time left over for his real job. And this veep isn't alone; nearly every working professional I've run across in the last few years faces a similar dilemma.

PIT TRICK: Give up trying to create the perfect résumé for every occasion.

What Use Are They?

If a potential employer has only thirty seconds to spend with your résumé and cover letter, then why should you even bother to create these documents? The answer is simple and pragmatic: They're your admission tickets into the job-hunting arena. Résumés and cover letters are the only acceptable responses to most help-wanted ads, and they're the currency you use when you network with other professionals who can help you in your reemployment efforts.

In any case, written pitches clearly serve employers' purposes, first and foremost. They enable employers to screen out candidates who lack the appropriate experience or knowledge, have spotty work records, or appear to have other weaknesses that would rule out their candidacy. On the other hand, if you want employers to consider you for a job, you have to play their game by sending them your résumé and cover letter. You can't avoid written pitches altogether, so think about the ways in which your résumé and cover letter can pay off. They just might help you open doors and at least give you an opportunity to get your foot inside.

Résumés and Cover Letters that Survive the Cut

Often, your written pitch is the only "voice" you have. You haven't yet spoken with a potential employer—and you won't get a chance to, either, unless you've crafted a résumé and cover letter that can survive the thirty-second countdown. That's why you need a pitch that's clear, simple, and to the point. In essence, it should say to the employer, "Here's how my qualifications and experience match your needs."

Remember, because your résumé and cover letter are necessarily one-sided—they represent a monologue rather than a dialogue with the employer—they must be able to stand entirely on their own. When the employer is glancing at your written pitch, you won't be there to clarify any information that's unclear, add any details that are missing, or turn around any objections that arise. But you can turn around what would otherwise be a disadvantage by customizing your written pitch for every employer you wish to contact and showing how your qualifications meet or exceed his or her needs.

PIT TRICK: Keep your written pitch short, to the point, and action-oriented.

Multiple Written Pitches

Because you have a your résumé and cover letter on a computer, it's easy enough to tailor them to meet each employer's requirements (you can determine these from the help-wanted ad you're answering, the company research you've conducted, or what you've heard from the person in your professional network who referred you). For example, if you know an employer is seeking candidates with ten years of management experience, then be sure your résumé and cover letter highlight your long-term management experience. It's perfectly acceptable to alter your written pitches to suit different situations, as long as you don't send more than one version of your résumé and cover letter to the same company (colleagues often share communications they receive from job hunters). Once you've found the core "professional you," you can serve it up in any way you want to meet the needs of an employer. You can change your objective, skills, the order of your qualifications, and other details on your résumés and cover letters, as the need arises, without compromising your integrity or your candidacy.

Caution: Employers may see hundreds of written pitches weekly, and they quickly develop a well-honed "B.S." detector. You won't be able to get away with exaggerating your qualifications or rewriting your work history very often, even if you're tempted to try. In order for your résumé and cover letter to be effective in most situations, they have to be truthful as well as believable. You should be able to stand behind your pitch effortlessly. If you're comfortable with every word of it, then chances are the employer will be, too; your ease with who you are and what you have to offer shines through. The most effective written pitch, therefore, always begins as an outgrowth of the inner work you've done (see Chapter 4) and a reflection of what you have learned about yourself. In fact, customizing your résumés and cover letters is a secondary consideration.

Guidelines for Crafting Résumés

At PIT meetings, we often exchange résumés and solicit members' feedback. And, of course, we see the results each week as PIT members discuss their ongoing marketing efforts. As I said earlier, there's no such thing as the perfect résumé. No PIT member, employment expert, or professional résumé writer I've talked to has discovered one writing style that's guaranteed to work all the time. But from my experience at PIT, I've been able to distill the writing techniques that seem to give résumés the best possible chance of surviving that thirty-second countdown:

- **Keep it short.** Fifteen years of solid work experience entitles you to a two-page résumé if you want one, but you're still probably better off keeping your résumé to one page. Remember, you don't have to itemize all your qualifications, no matter how impressive your work history may be. If you leave the employer wanting more information, he or she has to call you to get it. And that's exactly what you want in the first place: a phone call that gives you an opportunity to talk your way into an interview.
- **Keep it simple.** If you use technical terms that the reader may not understand or that slow the reader down, you'll probably succeed in turning off that individual—and relegating your résumé to the recycle pile.
- **Understand your options.** You can create either a chronological or a functional résumé, depending on your particular situation. The chronological résumé is the one that most employers are used to seeing, and it's therefore the one with which they probably feel most comfortable (and the one least likely to arouse their skepticism). However, if you've been unemployed for a while—especially if there have also been other gaps besides the current one in your work history—then a functional résumé may still be your best bet. It allows you to emphasize your experience rather than when you gained the experience.

■ **Front-load the most important information.** From the employer's point of view, whatever you open your résumé with—typically, your objective, skills, and most recent three jobs—is all that really counts. And that's probably the only thing he or she has time to look at in thirty seconds. You can therefore feel free to summarize your less significant work experience and place it farther down on the page.

■ **Quantify your most important accomplishments.** Adding such specifics as "increased sales by 20%" or "cut response time in half" helps bring your most important work experiences into focus and add to your credibility. Don't let modesty prevent you from singing your own praises; as long as the information you include is true and relevant, it's appropriate.

■ **Leave your personal life out of it.** The older you are, the less important your hobbies, group affiliations, and even your education become. Focus instead on the skills and experience that can best sell you to an employer. And never include your age or marital status; there's no possible payoff for you in including that information, and you certainly don't want to run the risk of being screened out because of it.

■ **Eliminate non-essential words.** After you write your résumé, go back and excise any information you don't absolutely need. Less is usually more, so present your qualifications in as few words as possible. Keep it crisp.

■ **Include only what feels comfortable.** You should be able to elaborate on your résumé when you're invited for an interview, so don't include any information, such as unpalatable or tedious job responsibilities, that you would be unwilling to discuss in person.

■ **Make it user-friendly.** Guide readers through the résumé by using bulleted points. Make it easy on the eyes by using generous margins and type that's large enough to be read without a magnifying glass. Don't clutter your résumé with a hodgepodge of fonts or an abundance of italics, boldfacing, and underlining. You want to create a clear and tasteful presentation, not a potential entry for a graphic design competition.

■ Enlist outside help. Ask people both in and out of your field to read your résumé. It should be understandable to lay people (such as the human resource professionals who are likely to get their hands on it first) as well as people who work in your field. Solicit feedback on the content before you send it to an employer, and also request that your readers check for typos, spelling, and grammatical errors.

Guidelines for Crafting Cover Letters

Now that you've created a résumé, it's time to write a complementary cover letter. Your cover letter, like your résumé, should be short and to the point. Its purpose is to establish a rapport with the potential employer and invite him or her to read your résumé. The cover letter shouldn't offer another description of your qualifications, nor should it contain the technical language you left out of your résumé.

There are actually two types of cover letters, both of which are intended for people you've never met. The first is used when you respond to classified ads; the second—for professionals to whom you were referred by members of your network—is intended to garner informational interviews.

When you're responding to an ad, your cover letter should answer these three questions for the reader:

■ Why are you writing to me?
■ What can you do to help me solve my problems?
■ What are your qualifications?

You should close your letter by asking when it would be convenient to arrange an interview.

By contrast, the cover letter you send when you're seeking an informational interview is a bit more comprehensive. It should open by telling the reader where you got his or her name—that's your hook. For example, you might begin the letter with "Dave Grayson and I were recently talking about niche marketing techniques, and he suggested I contact you." Your cover letter should then reassure the reader that you don't expect him or her to have a job or to know of one; you merely want to set up an informational meeting. And, as a courtesy, the letter should also tell the reader which questions you plan to raise during your interview. These might include:

- How did you get started in the industry?
- What do you like best and least about the industry?
- In your mind, what qualifications are required to be successful in the industry?
- How well would someone with my work experience fit into the industry?
- What are my résumé's strengths and weaknesses?

Again, close your cover letter with a request for a meeting. But because you're sending a warm cover letter instead of a cold response to a classified ad this time, you have a bit more control. Stress that you want the meeting to take place at a time and in a place that's convenient to the contact, and spell out the fact that you won't take up more than twenty minutes or so of his or her time. That shows your appreciation for the contact's busy schedule and makes the idea of meeting you more attractive.

As with résumés, cover letters always should be seen by at least one other set of eyes beside yours. Typos and other mistakes have a way of sneaking in, even when you use your computer's spell- and grammar-check features. Of course, anything less than a letter-perfect cover letter just isn't going to help you achieve your marketing goals.

Electronic Résumés and Cover Letters

Once you've created a résumé and cover letter that satisfy you and have met the scrutiny of your volunteer readers, it's time to consider whether or not your written pitch will survive the potential hazards of the electronic age. How do you know for sure that the résumé and cover letter you've generated will survive fax machines and electronic scanners? And why should you care?

It's quite likely at some point during your job search, someone will either fax your pitch or scan it into a computer. Sometimes this happens without your knowledge. Of course, you might consider faxing your résumé and cover letter yourself in response to help-wanted ads that provide fax numbers. Faxing your pitch could get it onto employers' desks immediately, and it certainly gets it there before the competition's arrive (assuming your competition uses snail-mail). It's also possible that a professional will want to fax your pitch to a colleague. The ease with which colleagues can fax information to one another might be to your advantage; it just might net you an unexpected interview opportunity with a potential employer. But that happens only if your résumé and cover letter are fax-friendly.

Similarly, your pitch might be scanned electronically into a company's database of job hunters. It's becoming increasingly common for employers to digitize résumés and cover letters instead of storing endless stacks of paper. Electronic résumés and cover letters have an advantage over paper beyond the space they save; employers can easily search them by computer to find candidates whose qualifications match a job opening. If you play your cards right, your written pitch can remain on file until the right job opportunity comes up. But again, you have to make sure your résumé and cover letter can survive the rigors of the scanning process.

You can make your written pitch both fax- and scanner- friendly if you follow my earlier advice and keep your résumé and cover letter simple. Although fax machines and scanners (and their accompanying OCR software) have become more sophisticated since the days when they could be counted on to periodically turn perfectly legible documents into unreadable garble, neither technology has reached the point where it can consistently keep every character on the page intact. However, there are some concrete steps you can take to ensure your résumé and cover letter glide easily through the high-tech gadgets:

■ **Recognize automation for what it is.** Scanning software and fax machines treat résumés and cover letters that don't conform to their electronic standards heartlessly and mindlessly, and you can't expect any more of them than that.

■ **Make it clear, not pretty.** Looking at an original document in hand, an employer's eye might be attracted by fancy typefaces, underlining, and italics. But these design elements won't fax or scan well. To minimize the risk, use a common font such as Courier or Times Roman that is easily recognized by most software. Also, avoid using type that's especially small or thin. And use white space rather than italics, boxes, and underlining to emphasize important information.

■ **Keep the contrast high.** Use white stationery and black print. The greater the difference between the background and foreground, the less likely your written pitch is to be garbled.

■ **Add keywords.** Even after your written pitch has been successfully scanned into a database, you still have one last challenge to overcome. Because employers electronically search for résumés and cover letters for job hunters whose qualifications match job openings, you have to "program" your written pitch in such a way that it turns up as often as possible. One way to do this is to add a section to the top of your résumé called "keywords" and then list all the terms you can think of for which an employer might search.

■ **Keep your résumés and cover letters as brief as you can.** If an employer has to scroll down the screen several times to finish reading your document, the reader might choose instead to move to the next pitch.

Despite your best efforts to keep your written pitch computer- and fax-friendly, it's still possible that a résumé and cover letter you've faxed will get lost en route to an employer's fax machine, or that a pitch you've sent will get garbled during the scanning process. So always follow up your faxed pitch with an original. If you know that an employer scans these documents into a computer—or you suspect there is a high probability that it does (larger companies are more likely than smaller ones to use the scanning process)—call the recipient to be sure your pitch was safely translated and stored.

PIT TRICK: Create bare-bones résumés and cover letters that glide through the automation process.

Help with Your Résumé and Cover Letter

You probably remember the basics of writing résumés and cover letters. However, if you want to refresh your memory or brush up on your technique, you'll find my favorite books on the topic in Appendix B. If you want more personal coaching, you'll find workshops on writing résumés and cover letters in your community; check the calendar section of your local newspaper to find out when and where they're held.

There's also software that can help you create résumés (and in some cases, cover letters). The programs typically include customizable résumé templates, and the more sophisticated packages feature a spellchecker, contact manager (for tracking employers' names, addresses, and critical dates), calendar, job-hunting or career management tips (either in the form of on-screen help or multimedia clips), and mail-merge functions (to personalize large-scale mailings). Check back issues of computer publications to find out which of the current software packages are the most highly rated. And when you visit a computer or software retail store, read packages carefully to be sure the software you're buying contains all the needed features and produces a technology-friendly document without unnecessary bells and whistles.

If you know that creating résumés and cover letters isn't your strong suit, you always have the option of hiring a professional writer. The cost of this service ranges upward from less than a hundred dollars, so don't just assume that you can't afford high-quality writing services. Check the phone book, and ask several candidates to send you samples of their work. It's worth investing in the help you need to create a written pitch with which you can feel comfortable. Your pitch, after all, forms the basis for the next leg of your job-hunting campaign.

PIT TRICK: When you're hiring a professional writer to refine your work, always draft your own résumé first; that way, you'll be able to stand behind everything that's on it.

Once you've created your résumé and cover letter, you can launch your marketing campaign. In the next chapter, you learn how PIT-tested networking techniques can help you tap into a wealth of unadvertised job opportunities. You also discover why informational interviewing may well be your quickest route to reemployment.

CHAPTER 7

The Shortest Path to Reemployment

Building a Network of Allies

You've sent out hundreds of résumés and cover letters, made the requisite follow-up phone calls, and landed several interviews. But the right job opportunity hasn't come along yet. Sure, your marketing approach—answering help-wanted ads and conducting mass mailings—may lead to a job offer eventually. But you're tired of waiting for the phone to ring, and you're burning to get back into the workplace as soon as possible. What can you do to accelerate the reemployment process? How can you cut through the red tape and sit down with knowledgeable professionals who can share insights, make connections happen, provide career feedback, and offer additional personal contacts that might help you find a job?

Speeding Up Your Job Search

You've probably heard of the miracle plant foods that help you grow bigger and sweeter tomatoes than you ever dreamed possible. Well, networking is the job-hunting equivalent of plant food, and reemployment is the fruit. Networking can dramatically increase your chances of being in the right place at the right time to harvest a job offer. Specifically, a job-hunting network helps you:

- Gain inside perspective about companies and your industry.
- Improve your presentation and rapport-building skills.
- Spread the word that you're in the job market.
- Garner personal introductions to other professionals.

Also, networking through informational interviewing lets you tap into the critical "hidden job market" that is invisible to most passive job seekers. Here's how three PIT members used their networking skills, particularly informational interviews, to unearth hidden job opportunities:

Joe, an unemployed copywriter, met with Roxanne, a senior account executive at an advertising company. She gladly referred him to professionals in other firms. But Roxanne also remembered Joe when the time came for her company to add several account executives to the payroll, and she offered him one of the newly created positions.

While Barbara was at an informational interview with a buyer at a local retail store, she learned about a management position that was about to be posted—for only two days—on a competing company's bulletin board. That was exactly the kind of job that Barbara was seeking, so she applied for the position within the narrow window of opportunity, and she was hired.

Alex received a telephone call from Dan, a financial analyst at a nonprofit organization, with whom he'd had an informational interview six weeks before. One of Dan's contacts, who worked at another nonprofit, had just asked Dan to be on the lookout for a potential corporate controller, and he immediately thought of Alex. Alex applied for, and was offered, the unadvertised position.

The stories of Joe, Barbara, and Alex aren't unique. In this chapter, I explain how to initiate the kind of bounce-back networking program that put them back on the job. First I guide you through the informational interviewing process, which is at the heart of networking. Then I show you how to maintain your job-hunting network so that it becomes a permanent part of your career success. Even when your job feels secure, it can only help you to have a network of industry allies who would move heaven and earth to help you maintain your career success.

The Golden Rules of Networking

Even when convinced of the invaluable benefits of networking, PIT members often doubt their abilities to build a network of contacts through informational interviewing. At the outset, they claim they're not friendly, gregarious, or aggressive enough to win the support of strangers who might be in a position to help them. But once they try it for themselves, they realize that informational interviewing works as long as they're willing to follow the Golden Rules of Networking:

■ Never ask networking contacts for a job.
■ Never expect networking contacts to have a job for you.
■ Never expect networking contacts to know of a job that would be right for you.

As I tell PIT members, if you want to win job-hunting allies, you have to *network with integrity*. Your primary task is to establish rapport during your informational interview, demonstrate a sincere desire to learn more about your contacts' career tracks, and ultimately learn how your qualifications might fit into your chosen industry.

If you approach networking honestly and with a willingness to listen and learn, you will go a long way toward building allies who can help you in your job search and beyond. But informational interviewing is not a game; if, at any point, you break one of the golden rules, then you might as well stop the process. By violating the trust of your contacts, you've compromised everyone in the network: the person you've affronted, the person who referred you to that person, the person who referred you to the person who referred you to that person, and so on. You've also forfeited your right to ask network members for their support.

PIT TRICK: Always network with integrity and honesty.

Prerequisite: Do Your Homework

Before you can begin the networking process and expedite your job search, you have to take care of a few preliminaries. First, adopt the right mindset by recognizing that your networking contacts gained through informational interviewing are not career counselors, and they're not responsible for helping you decide what kind of a job you want. In fact, they won't be able to help you unless you have a pretty good sense of what you want to do with the next phase of your career.

So complete your inner work (see Chapter 4) before you contact professionals and ask them to share their time with you. Also, take these steps to finish your pre-networking homework:

- Have a finished résumé and cover letter (see Chapter 6).
- Develop a clear job objective that you can verbally relay in a sentence or two, and be sure it reflects the goals you've highlighted in your written pitch.
- Know which companies interest you most.
- Know which professionals you most want to meet.

Finally, if you're switching careers, know enough about the industry you're trying to enter so that you can engage in intelligent shop talk. If you know where you're headed and what you want to do once you get there, you're likely to radiate confidence along with a clear sense of direction. Your winning attitude and sharp focus will impress your networking contacts and go a long way toward convincing them to lend you their support in your job search.

How to Begin Information Interviews

The building blocks of every network, large or small, are one-on-one informational interviews, or what most PIT members describe as the "fun part of unemployment." Unlike actual job interviews, which can be difficult to garner and often result in disappointment, informational interviews *always* lead to success. You may find some informational interviews more worthwhile than others, and you may stumble and make your share of mistakes along the way. But you never walk away from an informational interview empty-handed. Every informational interview teaches you something you can use in your job hunt and brings you a step closer to reemployment.

Because informational interviews are easy wins for most job hunters, I believe these meetings are more than worth all the time and energy you put into them. After all, you can't make too many friends in the working world or garner too many supporters. If at some point your job search feels stuck, you don't have to sit back and wait for the phone to ring. You always have the option of arranging an informational interview and talking to another professional who can give you new insights and perspective.

Informational interviews typically account for up to 80 percent of your working time while you're seeking reemployment, but there's no "right" number of informational interviews for every job seeker. I've seen some PIT members garner all the information they needed after just three or four meetings. Others continue the networking process over a period of months, with thirty or forty informational interviews.

Even if you know only a handful of potential contacts at the outset, don't worry; it only takes two or three good informational interviews to propel you through the networking process. Contacts beget contacts. In fact, most PIT members find that as they move closer to a job offer, the informational interviewing process speeds up. They find themselves meeting with a greater number of decision makers in a shorter time frame because, suddenly, they're in the loop. That, in a nutshell, is what informational interviews are all about.

Now let's look at each part of the informational interviewing process.

Why You Need Referrals

The world is filled with professionals who remember how hard it was to get a foot in the door at their companies or to establish a career in their industries. Many have experienced layoffs themselves at some point and feel a responsibility to help others who are in a similar position. Such people are often especially amenable to the idea of supporting others in their reemployment efforts. And nearly every professional feels flattered and inclined to help, if at all possible, when job seekers turn to him or her for *advice, not a job.*

Of course, busy professionals don't have the time to meet with everybody who requests an informational interview. I've found that most working people grant informational interviews first—and often exclusively—to job seekers referred to them by mutual acquaintances. Unsolicited written pitches or cold calls from job hunters, on the other hand, can sometimes land at the bottom of the work pile.

How to Begin

To get informational interviews, you need to have informational interviews. Sound like a Catch-22? It's not. You just need three contacts to launch your networking campaign. And everyone has at least three connections who can get the ball rolling. When I found myself out of work in 1990, I had just moved to the Winston-Salem area and knew virtually no one besides my family. But I was still able to find three people—my lawyer, a corporate president and CEO, and my priest—who were all willing to meet with me and could refer me to professionals in my field. Because they were well-respected members of my community and knew a great number of people, they provided a strong foundation upon which I was able to build my network.

Choose any successful and highly-regarded individuals in your community to begin your informational interviews. However, if you have the luxury of choosing from a wide range of possible primary contacts, I'd recommend that you select three people who know you well and whom you can trust. You're likely to feel awkward and fumble your way through your first round of informational interviews, and it's easiest—and safest—to make your mistakes early on in the process with people who are empathetic and provide helpful, positive feedback. Once you've polished your informational interviewing skills, there's no limit to how extensive your network can become.

At the Top

Ultimately, you want to network your way toward the most successful professionals in your industry who are willing to meet with you. These are the people who can best help you penetrate the hidden job market and get the word out that you're available for work. No one, no matter how high-ranking, is off limits to you as long as you can win a referral to him or her. Top-level managers, vice-presidents, and even CEOs can all be part of your networking efforts.

PIT TRICK: Create a networking plan that leads you to the most respected professionals in your field.

Landing an Informational Interview

Although it's generally possible to garner an informational interview once you have a referral, you still have to do the legwork. You should be able to set up informational interviews with your primary contacts easily enough: Perhaps all you'll have to do is pick up the phone and request a face-to-face meeting.

However, once your network extends beyond people already acquainted with you and you're soliciting secondary contacts, switching to a more formal approach is appropriate: the written pitch and verbal follow-up combination. Your written pitch should include a cover letter (that lets the reader know exactly who referred you and when you'll be calling to set up an interview), a résumé, and a list of interview questions (see Chapter 6). At the appointed day and time, follow up with a phone call to arrange a meeting.

Surviving the Telephone Screening Process

Even though you've prepared the secondary contact for your call, you still might find yourself screened by a gatekeeper—an administrative assistant or receptionist, or a voicemail system. In either case, begin your verbal pitch by mentioning the name of the person who referred you. You might say, for instance, "Denise Winters suggested that I call Mr. Hartley." Then explain that you're following up on a letter (and cite the date) that you previously sent.

Your task is to make it as easy as you can for whoever is screening your call to pass on the essentials about who you are and why you're calling (or if a voicemail system is screening your call, to deliver the message yourself efficiently and succinctly). At PIT, we suggest that if you have to leave a voicemail message, you spell your name, give your phone number twice, and state exactly when and where you'll be available by telephone so your potential contact can reach you. It is also perfectly appropriate to mention a date and time when you will try to reach the contact again.

You might be able to bypass the gatekeeper and voicemail system altogether if you call either before or after working hours, or during lunch. At these times, your potential contact might be more inclined to answer the phone. But don't count on it, and don't spend too much of your valuable time conducting pre-dawn and post-sunset sneak attacks. Many people screen their calls all the time and, if you want to reach them, you eventually have to deal with either a human or an electronic intermediary.

Other Timing Tips

Some days are better than others for rustling people up by telephone. In my experience, Wednesdays and Thursdays are the best days of the week for making follow-up calls. Mondays tend to be tough days to reach people because many of them are struggling to get back into the workday routine; Tuesdays are the heaviest mail days. On Fridays, people are usually in a rush to wind up their work so they can begin their weekends. Wednesdays and Thursdays tend to be the most relaxed, business-as-usual days of the week, and so they're the best days for phone calls.

However, the most important timing technique you have at your disposal is to follow up by phone exactly when you said you would in your letter. Even if you don't get the contact to come to the phone on your first try, you have demonstrated your reliability and increased your chances of a positive response.

PIT TRAP: Don't give up on potential contacts too soon or too easily; most of them are willing and eventually will be able to help you.

When They Don't Respond

If you don't hear back from the potential contact soon after you've called for the first time, don't despair. The person might be out of town or overwhelmed by work. Your phone message may have been garbled, or your original letter misplaced, so go about your business and call again at another time.

A tried-and-true PIT technique for reaching a professional who hasn't called you back after you've left a couple of messages is to send him or her a copy of your original letter. Write on the copy of the letter a short note explaining that your previous correspondence may have been lost. Suggest another day and time when you will call back, and then do so. You'll usually find a waiting and apologetic contact who's eager to make amends with you.

Most people to whom you're referred really do want to meet with you, and you should be able to arrange informational meetings with them if you're polite and persistent. Inevitably, though, you may run across one or two who just aren't willing to connect with you. If someone plays so hard to get that you find yourself leaving five unanswered messages, move on. You can't force somebody to grant you an informational interview, no matter who referred you. And even if you could, you wouldn't receive enough of a benefit from such a meeting to make it worth your time and effort. The good news is that there are enough professionals who want to meet with you that you don't have to agonize unduly over the one or two who "get away."

Setting Up a Meeting

When you finally engage your contact on the phone, your goal is to arrange an in-person meeting. Reiterate the promise that you made in your cover letter: You only need twenty minutes of the person's time. Still, that's a big chunk of time out of someone's day, so be sensitive to the potential contact's needs. If he or she wants to meet with you before or after business hours, be as flexible as you can.

Your potential contact might even want to conduct the informational meeting outside the office—say, in an airport or a restaurant. Such a meeting, of course, doesn't give you the opportunity to get a firsthand look at the business and pick up clues about the company's culture. But if an informational interview outside the office is the only kind that fits into the contact's schedule, agree to it.

There's only one point on which you shouldn't waiver: You want to conduct your informational interview in person rather than by phone. There are a couple of reasons for this. First of all, you want to observe your contact so you can communicate effectively. What someone says and what his or her body language tells you may be two different things. Second, an informational interview is, in a sense, a dress rehearsal for a job interview. You want your networking contact's feedback on how well you present yourself during the interview, and you can only get that feedback from an in-person meeting.

At the Meeting

Because an informational interview is similar to a job interview, many of the same rules apply. Be on time (which actually means be ten or fifteen minutes *early*) and dress formally, as though you were trying to convince someone to hire you. Also, come prepared with a notebook and pen, and have handy your own copy of the questions you mailed in advance to your contact.

Your primary goal in an informational interview is to establish rapport with the other person and to make a friend who will want you to succeed in your job search. You also want a decision-maker's perspective on how you fit into the big picture. Be willing to listen to and learn from what the professional has to say, even if it isn't what you hoped to hear.

Use the questions you've brought with you to launch your conversation. As I said earlier in the book, these might include:

- How did you get started in the industry?
- What do you like best and least about the industry?
- In your mind, what qualifications are required to be successful in the industry?
- How well would someone with my work experience fit into the industry?
- What are my résumé's strengths and weaknesses?

But no matter how carefully you've fashioned your questions, you'll want to be flexible to some extent. If your contact goes off on a tangent because one of your questions especially interests him or her, enjoy the opportunity to travel down the new path and glean the additional information. Every informational interview is unique, and you can maximize the potential of each by staying receptive to the contact's interests and conversational preferences.

Remember, too, that you might have some information that would be valuable to your contact. Although you're there to learn from your interviewer, you may have the opportunity to teach the interviewer something, too. Take advantage of it. A two-way dialogue gives you a chance to help your contact; thus, it may cement your professional relationship and benefit you more than if you remain entirely on the receiving end of the information exchange.

PIT TRICK: Stay flexible enough during the informational interview to take advantage of spontaneous learning—and teaching—opportunities.

Saying Goodbye

If you establish a rapport with your interviewer and keep the conversation flowing, time passes quickly. So keep an eye on the clock, and always let the contact know when twenty minutes have passed and it's time for you to leave. I've found that, often, the conversation is just getting started after twenty minutes. The contact might invite you to stay a bit longer, in which case you should. But if twenty minutes is all the time you get, that should still be long enough to ask your questions and accomplish your two final goals.

Your first goal is to request feedback on your presentation. Find out what your strengths and weaknesses are from your interviewer's perspective. You can then modify your delivery for the next interview.

Your second goal is to walk away with the names of two or three other professionals that the interviewer feels comfortable referring you to for additional informational interviews. If your interviewer is undecided about whom you should connect, ask whether you can check back in a day or two. Reemphasize the Golden Rules of Networking, especially that you won't ask anyone to whom you're referred for a job; you simply want to get his or her perspective on how you might fit into the workplace. If your contact wants to refer you to others who work in his or her company, all the better. You'll have a chance to see the organization from different vantage points and learn even more about it. If not, accept your contact's judgment about which referrals would benefit you the most, and gratefully continue the networking process.

Following Through

As soon as possible after your meeting, jot down notes to help you remember what you've discussed. That night, write a thank-you note. If you received potential contact names during the interview, write cover letters to these professionals and include the copies with your thank-you letter (or, if you get referrals during a subsequent phone conversation, send copies of the letters under separate cover as soon as you can). This shows a strong sense of urgency, and it demonstrates both how much you valued your meeting and your eagerness to follow through on your contact's advice right away. Also, send copies of all your correspondence to as many of your downstream contacts— say, two or three meetings removed from the present—as you reasonably can. This keeps your name in front of your most recent contacts and tells them you're still enthusiastically pursuing your career goals and networking opportunities.

After the Interview

Use an efficient filing system to keep track of your growing network. You may use contact-management software if you've already invested in it, but I've seen PIT members set up equally efficient systems with a binder, index cards, or manila folders. In any case, include in your records the notes you jotted down immediately after the interview as well as vital contact information (the date of your meeting, who referred you, and the like). That enables you to keep a permanent record of your job-hunting allies and makes it easy to stay in contact with them. Once you're reemployed, send everyone in your files a letter announcing the good news and expressing your gratitude for his or her help.

Even after you're well established in your new job, you might still call members of your network or send them a letter (or perhaps an interesting article or copies of any publication or trade paper that quotes or mentions you) occasionally to keep in touch. Over the years, you may add to your network or focus on several core members with whom you want to maintain the closest contact. In any event, as long as you take the time to nourish it, your network will take care of you for the rest of your career.

PIT TRICK: Nurture your network, and it will nuture you.

Random but Wonderful

The interesting thing about networking is that you never know exactly where it will lead or whom you'll meet. You simply take cues from your interviewers and flow from one networking opportunity to another. But just because you can't control the process of networking doesn't mean you can't enjoy it.

In fact, many PIT members tell me that networking gives them the opportunity to talk with high-powered people—busy professionals at the top rungs of their industries' career ladders—whom they otherwise would never have an opportunity to meet. One PIT member even confessed that he enjoyed networking so much he wished he could do it for a living. Networking can be an exciting and uplifting by-product of the reemployment process for you, too, if you choose to see it that way.

Once you're comfortable with informational interviews, it's time to prepare for the real thing: job interviews. In the next chapter, you learn about the differences between informational interviews and job interviews. In addition, you discover how even job interview "failures" can contribute to a career bounce-back success.

CHAPTER 8

Cheek-to-Cheek, Pen-to-Paper

Finessing Every Interview and Negotiation

Your networking campaign is moving ahead at warp speed, and you're feeling increasingly proficient at informational interviewing. But you still worry about the thought of enduring a job interview. Is there any way to transfer your informational interviewing skills to the job-interview arena? And if you do impress an interviewer enough to garner a job offer, how can you decide whether you should accept it, negotiate for a higher salary, or keep searching for a better opportunity?

The Final Frontier

Through your networking experience, you've likely become an expert at informational interviews. But no one I know has ever received a job offer solely on the basis of an informational interview. If you want to rejoin the workforce, you have to learn how to handle yourself at job interviews as confidently and impressively as you do at informational interviews. Unfortunately, this is precisely the point at which many PIT members falter. Many job seekers with whom I've worked—even those who admit to enjoying informational interviews—are so intimidated by decision makers who seem to have life-and-death power over their careers that they willingly give up control of the job interview to them. This passivity and indecisiveness only serve to scare potential employers out of hiring them (it's hard to imagine hiring job candidates who tremble with fear during interviews) and needlessly prolong their job searches.

Throughout this book, I've stressed the fact that the PIT job-hunting program is a proactive one. This is as true during the final stage of your reemployment efforts—the job interview—as it is during the earlier stages. If you take charge of the job interview and follow the career bounce-back job interview guidelines in this chapter, you stand out from the crowd of nervous applicants and are more likely to win a job offer. Furthermore, you're also in a better position to determine whether or not you even want the job.

In the following pages, I explain how to conduct take-charge job interviews that maximize your chances of reemployment. I also share bounce-back techniques for assessing the job offers you receive in the context of whether or not they match your career goals. And I show you how to negotiate the highest possible starting salary and benefits for job offers that make your personal final cut.

The Right Mindset

Your ultimate goal, of course, is to get a job offer. Even more important, you're trying to win the *right* job offer. It doesn't help you to impress the socks off an interviewer who has a job that doesn't match your skills, preferences, and needs. And there's no need to feel bad when you don't garner the wrong job offer. Just tell yourself that it was the best possible decision for all parties, and then move on.

During my own reemployment efforts, I interviewed for what sounded like a terrific job in the retail industry. I spent eight hours proving to half a dozen affable interviewers that I was eminently qualified for the position. Because the interview seemed to have gone exceedingly well and I wanted to show my enthusiasm for the job, I used an overnight courier to send six thank-you letters. A week later, the executive recruiter with whom I was working called to say, "They loved you, but they're going to fill the position from within the company." I asked her where I'd gone wrong, and she confessed that no one had ever Fed-Ex'd thank-you letters to the company before. "You showed real creativity," she explained, "and that was a problem for them. The position requires someone who isn't creative, doesn't 'rock the boat' with new ideas, and is content with rigid routine. Your initiative took you out of the running." Later, as I processed the feedback, my initial disappointment gave way to elation. "Yes, I am creative," I thought to myself with a sense of satisfaction, "and I certainly don't want to suppress that important element of myself for the sake of getting a job." The fact is, every job I've ever held has challenged me to think on my feet, and I'd be miserable if I were stuck in any other type of position. So to this day, I feel grateful to that company for not hiring me and potentially saving me from years of drudgery and unhappiness in a job that wouldn't have been a good match for me after all.

Transferable Interviewing Skills

If you want to take charge of a job interview so that you can decide if the job requirements match yours, you have to use the listening skills you acquired during your informational interviews. You also need the focus, self-confidence, and enthusiasm you brought to the networking process. Finally, never forget that your mission during the job interview is same as it was during your informational interviews: to establish rapport with the interviewer. You win allies in the professional world by listening to what they have to say and asking intelligent questions to keep the conversation flowing, and you impress the interviewer. In short, even though your immediate goal for the interview has shifted from networking to reemployment, the skills that you need to finesse the interview are still the same.

Solving the Problem

Every interviewer wants to know one thing: whether or not you're the solution to the company's problems. Do you have the skills and the personality to match the employer's needs, and are you willing to use them in this position? You learn if you are indeed the solution to the problem by watching and listening.

Be attuned to the interviewer's body language, and what you can learn from the office itself. For example, a harried employer with a messy office might be looking for someone with great organizational skills. Conversely, a laid-back interviewer whose golf clubs conspicuously adorn a corner of the office might want an upbeat associate who is an asset to the team.

Once you've assessed the visual clues available, actively listen to what the employer is saying to glean additional insights into his or her needs. Then frame your answer to the interview questions in terms of the employer's requirements. You might say, "You're looking for somebody with strong management skills. In my last position, I supervised a staff of six, and I was in charge of hiring and firing for my department."

If you're not seeing or hearing enough information to be sure what the interviewer is looking for, ask for clarification. You can restate the interviewer's question to make sure you've understood it and take a moment or two to get your thoughts together. Then, when you feel confident enough to continue, you can answer the question. In that way, you can demonstrate not only your listening skills but also your ability to stay calm under pressure. Also, before you respond to an open-ended question or statement such as "Tell me about yourself," be sure you've pinned down exactly what information the interviewer wants to hear.

PIT members often meet interviewers who seem uncomfortable with the interviewing process. When this happens, I advise them to gently take charge and establish structure by asking questions that help clarify the interview's purpose. By asking questions such as, "Are we discussing a specific job opportunity within your company?" PIT members have discovered that they can establish structure for the interview and align themselves with the interviewer's goals.

Just as you brought along a list of questions to ask at informational interviews, it's appropriate to prepare reasonable queries for all job interviewers, no matter what their interviewing skills may be. Questions like the following help you get to the heart of the employer's concerns and needs:

- What would my exact job responsibilities be?
- How, specifically, does this job (and the department) relate to the company?
- Is this a newly created position?
- If not, what happened to the person who previously held this position?
- If he or she was promoted, what were the things that enabled that person to move through this organization?

Once the interviewer fills in the blanks for you, you have a better sense of what the job requires and whether you can bring the necessary skills, experience, and qualities to the table. You're also in a good position to discuss how you tackled similar challenges in the past. Share a related anecdote or two with the interviewer. It not only demonstrates that you were listening but also gives you a chance to show yourself as someone with the experience to handle the job.

PIT TRICKS: During the initial interview, address the employer's critical concerns: "Will you fit into the organization's culture? Can you provide leadership now and in the future? Are you motivated to do the job?"

Project a Winning Attitude

An interview question that derails many PIT members is "What are your weaknesses?" I tell them that for the purposes of the job interview, they have no weaknesses—only strengths they've restated as weaknesses to satisfy the interviewer's question. For example, you might say your biggest weakness is that you like to get the job done well, or that you demand perfection from yourself in everything you do. By genuinely admitting to any actual weaknesses, you take yourself off the short list of job candidates.

Why? Well, aren't we all fallible? Sure. But everything is in the packaging and presentation. All interviewers, regardless of the job in question or the industry involved, want to hire winners. Their reputation depends on it. So your task is to project a winning attitude—that is, an understanding of your purpose in life and assurance that you can handle whatever arises along the way.

PIT TRAP: Never bite the baited hook by admitting to any major weaknesses.

Many human resources professionals tell me that, first and foremost, they look for a "winner's spark" in the job candidate's eye. If you're charged with positive energy and a can-do attitude, the interviewer sees that glint of self-assurance. So before your job interview, meditate on your past successes (reread your résumé if you need to jog your memory), and take the time to mentally pat yourself on the back for all that you've done. You may have accomplished the equivalent of parting the Red Sea in your career, but that only works to your advantage during the job interview if you feel great about your accomplishment. If all you managed was simply "another" Red Sea parting, which anyone in your position could have done, then you might as well forget about using the accomplishment to impress your interviewer. First you must impress yourself as a winner.

Naturally, another characteristic of winners is that they get to interviews at least fifteen minutes early. If you have any doubt about the length of time needed to get to the employer's office or any questions about directions, ask—or make a dry run beforehand. Dress professionally for every interview, regardless of where or with whom you're meeting. Even advertising agencies, graphic design firms, and other businesses whose employees may be on the cutting edge of fashion expect job candidates to dress for success. Once you've been hired, you can dress to blend in with the company's "unique" culture; until then, your task is to appear well groomed and businesslike from the moment you walk through the employer's door.

A winning attitude and appearance also may help you overcome any perceived shortcomings in your qualifications. Winners project a confidence in their ability to learn anything they don't yet know, and an inner belief that they can successfully work with anyone on the team. And because winners prefer to associate with other winners, employers are naturally drawn to job candidates who radiate confidence in their prior accomplishments and their present-day qualifications, and belief in their future success.

PIT TRICK: Prepare for tough interview questions by rehearsing your answers ahead of time.

Your Needs

To a large extent, employers rely on their first impressions of you when they make their hiring decisions. If you appear to be the kind of person with whom they'd like to work, then you're ten steps ahead of the competition. Your qualifications often matter less than how well the employer responds to you personally. If you're the job candidate the employer is drawn to, then you have an edge even if other applicants have more job-related experience.

Similarly, you can gauge very quickly how well your personality meshes with the interviewer's. Your opinion of the job, and its suitability for you, may be influenced by the people you encounter before, during, or after the interview, or by the office itself. You can't help responding to the interview at an emotional level, just as the employer has no choice but to react subjectively to you.

As I said earlier, you're in control of the job interview, just as you are of the entire PIT bounce-back process. That means, in part, you don't have to accept any job offer that doesn't feel right to you. But regardless of what your intuition tells you about the job during your interview, keep an open mind. Your needs and preferences are critical, but they should be on the back burner until you've been offered the job.

Finally, don't forget that the employer has called you to arrange the interview and is therefore in a greater power position than the people you contact to set up informational interviews. But as stressed earlier in this book, this doesn't mean you have to give up all control to the employer. You always want to retain as much control of the job interview as you can. To that end, keep your interest in the position and "court" the employer until there's an offer on the table and you have to make a decision.

Your Expectations

When you conducted informational interviews, you knew the probable outcome: with a little luck, you'd add additional contacts to your growing job-hunting network. Still, I encounter new PIT members every week who believe the goal of job interviews is equally clear: to get the job offer. Before long, though, they realize that it just isn't the case. Your ultimate goal in interviewing is to get *the job that's meant for you.* At the same time, it's important to keep in mind that your first interview with a potential employer rarely leads to a job offer, whether or not the position is a match for you. If you play your cards right, though, a first job interview leads to an invitation for a second interview. A second interview may lead to an invitation for a third, and so on, until the employer has made up his or her mind.

During the first job interview, your task is to provide enough information to interest the employer in continuing a dialogue with you at another time. Don't overwhelm the employer by spilling your life story. Keep your answers as brief as possible. Always leave the employer wanting more information about you—which, of course, you'll be happy to provide during a future interview.

Second Interview and Beyond

If you've established great rapport with the interviewer, then you can expect to be called in for a second interview. The employer will call you on his or her timetable, regardless of how anxious you are. In the meantime, your task is to write a thank-you letter to the interviewer (and to anyone else who took time to meet with you), and to send copies to the two or three people immediately downstream in your network. Then forge ahead with your job search, and forget about the interview for the moment. Otherwise, you'll drive yourself crazy, or perhaps do something rash and jeopardize your chances of getting the job.

This brings us to a related point. Many job seekers who have a good feeling about a first interview convince themselves that reemployment is just around the corner. They sit beside the telephone and wait for it to ring. Then, as the days (and sometimes weeks) go by with no word from the employer, they become discouraged. They may feel rejected and slip back into the e-wave cycle (see Chapter 2), thus slowing their reemployment efforts.

I can attest from my own reemployment experience, and from listening to hundreds of PIT members, that not hearing from an interviewer when you expected to doesn't mean you've been bypassed for the job. If you think the interview was a success, you may be right; the employer's enthusiasm for you hasn't necessarily waned. The interviewer may be traveling, or a pressing business crisis may have erupted in the workplace. Remember: When you're not working, your sense of time is different from that of working professionals. You're not the only person, or the most important one, on the interviewer's mind; the interviewer has many other pressing responsibilities besides hiring. I tell PIT members that it's not uncommon for busy professionals to be several weeks behind on non-critical correspondence (which includes hiring). Even under the best circumstances, two or three weeks often elapse between interviews. So stay optimistic and assume that you're still in the running for the job until you receive word to the contrary.

While you're waiting to hear, stay focused and continue your job-hunting campaign. Use the time between interviews to continue your marketing efforts and, if possible, garner other job offers. Set up informational interviews, stay in touch with recruiters, respond to classified ads, proceed with your mailings and follow-up calls, chat with other professionals in cyberspace, and keep doing all the other things that have been part of your career bounce-back mission. In short, continue your all-out job search until you accept an offer.

Note that it is appropriate to call and request an update on the position if the employer hasn't called you by an agreed-upon date. Don't put off calling because you're afraid to receive bad news. If the interviewer has already decided against hiring you, you can't make the situation any worse by remaining uninformed about the choice. Besides, hearing the final decision provides you with closure and gives you an opportunity to get valuable feedback. When I was out of work and about to make a follow-up call, I would ask myself: "Hey, what's the worst thing that could happen? They can't fire me, because I'm already unemployed. All they can do is say no." That always made it easier to pick up the phone.

Moving on After Rejection

An interviewer who doesn't hire you has even more to teach you than one who does. If you receive a rejection either by telephone or letter, follow the PIT-tested procedure of asking the employer for feedback.

When you call an interviewer who rejected you, always find out what he or she liked best, and least, about your presentation. I also advise PIT members to find out whether there was a specific reason why the interviewer chose not to hire them. Listen and learn from the criticism, and then move on.

Sometimes, your follow-up efforts might win unexpected allies for you. For example, the last time I was out of work I called an employee who'd decided not to hire me, to find out why. She explained that she had bypassed me to rehire a former employee with whom she had proven rapport. During our conversation, she offered valuable feedback about my personal presentation style and encouraged me to keep in touch with her. In taking that advice, I gained a strong advocate who continued to send job leads and make connections for me throughout my campaign.

One thing is certain at this point: Rejection doesn't mean you "failed" the interview and that if you follow a specific set of guidelines, you'll score a job the next time around. Rejection has nothing to do with your abilities or your intrinsic value as an employee. Instead, it simply has to do with that one decision maker's preferences and perceptions. The next employer might hire you for the very same reasons this interviewer chose not to! Every job search brings with it rejection after rejection. Your challenge is to rise above the rejection and continue your bounce-back efforts until you land in the workplace again.

PIT TRICK: Turn job-hunting rejections into networking opportunities.

The Job Offer

Beginning with the second interview, your goal is to snare the job offer. To do this, work on enhancing the relationship you've developed with the employer. Continue to listen to what the employer has to say, and focus on reinforcing the idea that you're the one candidate who can meet his or her needs.

If the subject of money comes up before the employer has clearly indicated that he or she is ready to make you a firm offer, politely sidestep the issue. If you pursue the topic, the interviewer might sense your anxiety or desperation and try to hire you "on the cheap." Or if the starting salary you're after exceeds the figure the employer had in mind, you might actually talk yourself out of a job. Either way, a premature discussion about money for a job you haven't been offered is never to your advantage.

How do you forestall talking about compensation? Simple. Tell the interviewer that you'll be in a better position to talk about salary when you learn more about the job or explain that money is less of an issue for you than whether or not the position is a match for you. Emphasize your certainty that you can negotiate a fair offer once you've determined that both you and the employer are headed down the same road. An interviewer who is seriously considering you for employment respects your right to postpone a discussion about salary until the time is right.

With luck, the second interview ends with a job offer. But many PIT members have been invited back for third, fourth, and even fifth interviews before they're asked to join the staff. The process can take a while, but it does come to an eventual end with either a rejection or a job offer. We've already discussed the former. Now it's time to consider the latter.

Negotiation

Once you've been unemployed for a while, any job offer can look like the answer to your prayers. I've seen too many PIT members jump ecstatically at the first offer they receive without attempting to sweeten the compensation pot. Even after job hunters know that the interviewer is sold on the idea of hiring them, they don't understand the power of their position. They're afraid of appearing greedy if they ask for more compensation than the employer has offered. And they fear that, in the worst case, the employer will be turned off at the prospect of haggling over money and will withdraw the offer.

In my experience, the worst never happens. There's no risk I can detect that goes along with negotiating for the compensation you deserve. Sure, you can assume that most employers are honest and will do their best to name a fair salary. But that rarely represents the highest figure the employer is willing to—or even expects to—pay. When you can't wring any more cash out of the deal, you can often procure bonuses, stock options, vacation time, and other perks to sweeten the deal.

Whatever you do, don't sell yourself short in your eagerness to get back to work. You deserve the best compensation package that you can negotiate. Over the course of your career, even a seemingly insignificant difference between the salary you earn and what you could have obtained will add up. If the interviewer has made you an offer, you've proven your value to the employer. You owe it to yourself, your future, and your family to negotiate the best possible deal for your services and loyalty to the company.

Evaluating the Job

Assuming you and the employer are able to agree on a fair salary and benefits package, it's time to decide whether or not to take the plunge. You don't have to accept the job offer until you've determined, to the best of your ability, that it's the right career move for you. Some PIT members quickly graduate into new positions, only to reappear at a meeting months later because they're unemployed again. They usually must begin the career bounce-back process anew—beginning with dealing with their shock and anger.

The lesson to be learned from them is this: Resist the temptation to accept the first offer that comes your way just because it's an easy way to put an end to your job search. Before you commit to another workplace experience, be sure that your instincts tell you it's a good move. If anything about the job seems off to you, *take those inner signals very seriously.* Trust your gut—it's an invaluable barometer of happiness and success. Take the time to match what the position has to offer against your needs and preferences, and be honest with yourself. The right job is worth waiting for, and your first job offer is certainly not going to be your last. You *will* find the job that's right for you, if you stay in charge of your quest for reemployment. Your instincts will tell you when you've arrived at your destination.

The Career Bounce-Back! Program™ is an emotionally charged, wild journey. But for those who stick with it, there is almost always a happy ending.

Remember Frank, the PIT member and reemployed industrial engineer we met in the introduction? In the eighteen months since he celebrated his PIT graduation, he's been promoted several times and is now a vice-president. He's also joined the PIT advisory board and has become a familiar face at our weekly meetings.

"While I was unemployed, I often had to drag myself to PIT meetings," he recently confessed to the group of mostly newcomers who had joined since his graduation. "But luckily for me, I stuck with it. I wouldn't be where I am today if it hadn't been for the support, camaraderie, and perspective of PIT members. I know it will work for you, too, if you believe in the program and take a proactive approach to reemployment."

APPENDIX A

PIT's Top Ten Guerrilla Job-Hunting Tactics

Cutting Edge Strategies from Members of PIT Support Groups

From the moment I began writing this book, I knew the project would be complete only if it included the best of PIT members' guerrilla job-hunting tactics. These cutting-edge strategies were cited time and time again as the reasons why PIT members had landed their jobs. So I turned to PIT members for their help in compiling this section. As you can see, they came through.

For six months, I brought a notebook with me each week to PIT meetings. At each session's end, I asked PIT members and PITAs (Professionals In Transition Alumni) to share the precise reemployment techniques that had worked for them, and I jotted down their answers. Then I distilled the responses into PIT's Top Ten Guerrilla Job-Hunting Tactics.

TACTIC 1: *Remind Yourself to Be a Winner*

Reinforce your winning attitude by posting "attitude" signs (with whatever motto works for you—several PIT members simply use the single word *attitude*) in visible places such as your daily planner, the bulletin board or wall in your temporary office, or even on top of your bureau. The signs remind you that you alone are responsible for your daily attitude.

TACTIC 2: *Conduct a Multi-level Campaign*

Your reemployment effort consists of three parts: working with job-hunting allies (recruiters, career consultants, and the like), marketing yourself, and conducting informational interviews. You're not finished with any aspect of your campaign until you've accepted a job offer; instead, keep juggling all the marketing balls at once throughout the reemployment process.

TACTIC 3: *Create a Business Card*

Don't be left out of the old introduction ritual of exchanging business cards just because you're unemployed. In fact, you need a card now more than ever. So create one and have it professionally printed. Include your name, contact information, and general area of expertise. On the back, add your career objective and a bulleted list of your key areas of strength; your business card then can actively serve as a mini-résumé.

TACTIC 4: *Meet Employers' Needs*

When you're responding to a help-wanted advertisement, design a cover letter that proves you're the answer to the employer's problems. Cull those problems from the ad, and list them in the left-hand column of your cover letter under the heading "Your Needs." Then itemize your matching requirements in a right-hand column entitled "My Qualifications." This minimalist cover-letter style lets employers see, at a glance, that you're qualified for the job.

TACTIC 5: Use Large Mailing Envelopes

Most job hunters mail their résumés and cover letters in number ten envelopes. Instead, use catalogue envelopes (9" x 12" or 10" x 15"). In doing so, your written pitch stands out from the others right from mail delivery, and your résumés and cover letters are more likely to arrive in pristine condition. Finally, your résumés and cover letters are easier for employers to scan, fax, and photocopy if never folded.

TACTIC 6: Volunteer

Helping others is an excellent way to help yourself. As one PIT member who volunteers at a community soup kitchen puts it: "I have no idea where my next dollar is coming from, but at least I can give of myself." You connect with others, some of whom might potentially help you in your job search, and gain a new perspective on your problems. Even while experiencing rough times in your career, there are always people who are facing even greater challenges in life.

TACTIC 7: Get Out and Meet People

If there's ever a time to be a shrinking violet, this isn't it. You need advocates in your job search, and you can find them practically anywhere. So get in front of as many people as possible. Join civic and religious groups, participate in community events, attend support group meetings (you'll find listings in your local business journal), and renew your ties with your college's alumni association. It's a good way to build your networking skills and advance your job search.

TACTIC 8: Recruit a Coach

Find a personal advocate, other than a spouse or other family member, who can hold your hand and provide "tough love" throughout the reemployment process. This person should be compassionate and understand you, someone with whom you can always speak freely. Your coach's job is to encourage you, pick you up by your bootstraps when you need it, and obtain frequent job-search progress reports from you.

TACTIC 9: Keep a Journal

Keep a written record of your day-to-day reemployment efforts. You can spot trends and learn from any emerging job-search patterns. You can also write about your unemployment-related feelings and concerns, which is a terrific way to get them off your chest. In addition, your job-search journal might produce some spontaneous problem-solving ideas and insights.

TACTIC 10: Stay Proactive

You can control your job search, but it's *your* choice to search, and yours alone. There are reemployment possibilities everywhere; you just have to go out and find them. When opportunity doesn't knock, build a door. Don't let your job search stall while you wait for a headhunter or an employer to call. Instead, turn the situation around. Line up informational interviews and keep the reemployment process moving. Above all, remember that reemployment is a personal responsibility and a proactive process.

The Essential Eclectic Library

Helpful Books, Magazines, and Other Resources

Where do PIT members turn between meetings when they need some bounce-back inspiration? To the Professionals In Transition library, almost all the contents of which presently reside at our home office.

In the following pages, you'll find career-related tomes from the library as well as other resources that are helpful for professionals in transition. Several are likely to help you through various stages of the reemployment and healing process.

Magazines

The Best Small Companies in America
Forbes, Inc.
60 5th Avenue
New York, NY 10011
(800) 888-9896

The Inc. 500 Issue
   The Goldhirsh Group
   38 Commercial Wharf
   Boston, MA 02110
   (800) 234-0999

Fortune's Top Industrial 500 and *Top Service 500*
   Time, Inc.
   Time/Life Building, Rockefeller Center
   New York, NY 10020-1393
   (800) 621-8000

National Business Employment Weekly
   Dow Jones & Co.
   200 Liberty Street
   New York, NY 10281
   (800) 562-4868

Career Books

Beat the Odds: Career Buoyancy Tactics for Today's Turbulent Job Market
   Martin Yate
   Ballantine Books
   201 E. 50 Street
   New York, NY 10022
   (212) 751-2600

Career Anchors: Discovering Your Real Values and Guide
   Edgar H. Schein
   Pfeiffer & Co.
   350 Sansome Street
   San Francisco, CA 94104
   (800) 274-4434

Career Bounce-Back! Reemployment Toolbox workbook
   J. Damian Birkel
   Career Bounce-Back! Publishing
   Box 11252
   Winston-Salem, NC 27116-1252
   (336) 757-1099

Cover Letters for Dummies
  Joyce Lain Kennedy
  IDG Books Worldwide, Inc.
  919 E. Hillsdale Boulevard, Suite 400
  Foster City, CA 94404
  (800) 762-2974

Cover Letters That Knock 'em Dead
  Martin Yate
  Adams Publishing
  260 Center Street
  Holbrook, MA 02343
  (617) 767-8100

Damn Good Résumé Guide
  Yana Parker
  Ten Speed Press
  Box 7123
  Berkeley, CA 94707
  (510) 559-1600

Do What You Are: Discover the Perfect Career for You
Through the Secrets of Personality Type
  Paul D. Tieger and Barbara Barron-Tieger
  Little, Brown and Company, Inc.
  34 Beacon Street
  Boston, MA 02108
  (800) 343-9204

Electronic Job Search Revolution
  Joyce Lain Kennedy
  John Wiley & Sons, Inc.
  605 Third Avenue
  New York, NY 10158
  (212) 850-6000

Electronic Résumé Revolution:
Creating a Winning Résumé for the New World of Job Seeking
  Joyce L. Kennedy and Thomas J. Morrow
  John Wiley & Sons, Inc.
  605 Third Avenue
  New York, NY 10158
  (212) 850-6000

Guerrilla Tactics in the New Job Market
   Tom Jackson
   Bantam Books
   1540 Broadway
   New York, NY 10036
   (800) 223-6834

Is Your "Net" Working?
A Complete Guide to Building Contacts and Career Visibility
   Anne Boe and Bettie B. Youngs
   John Wiley & Sons, Inc.
   605 Third Avenue
   New York, NY 10158
   (212) 850-6000

It's Never Too Late: 150 Men and Women Who Changed Their Careers
   Robert K. Otterbourg
   Barrons Educational Series, Inc.
   250 Wireless Boulevard
   Hauppauge, NY 11788
   (800) 645-3476

Job and Career Building
   Richard Germann and Peter Arnold
   Ten Speed Press
   Box 7123
   Berkeley, CA 94707
   (510) 559-1600

JobBank
   Adams Publishing
   260 Center Street
   Holbrook, MA 02343
   (617) 767-8100

Job Hunting for Dummies
   Max Messmer
   IDG Books Worldwide, Inc.
   919 E. Hillsdale Boulevard, Suite 400
   Foster City, CA 94404
   (800) 762-2974

Job Interviews for Dummies
Joyce Lain Kennedy
IDG Books Worldwide, Inc.
919 E. Hillsdale Boulevard, Suite 400
Foster City, CA 94404
(800) 762-2974

Knock 'em Dead: With Great Answers to Tough Interview Questions
Martin Yate
Adams Publishing
260 Center Street
Holbrook, MA 02343
(617) 767-8100

Occupational Outlook Handbook
Katherine G. Abraham and Robert B. Reich
JIST Works, Inc.
720 N. Park Avenue
Indianapolis, IN 46202-3431
(800) 648-5478

Résumés for Dummies
Joyce Lain Kennedy
IDG Books Worldwide, Inc.
919 E. Hillsdale Boulevard, Suite 400
Foster City, CA 94404
(800) 762-2974

Résumés That Knock 'em Dead
Martin Yate
Adams Publishing
260 Center Street
Holbrook, MA 02343
(617) 767-8100

Secrets of Savvy Networking
Susan Roane
Warner Books, Inc.
1271 Avenue of the Americas
New York, NY 10301
(212) 522-7200

Sweaty Palms: The Neglected Art of Being Interviewed
　　H. Anthony Medley
　　Ten Speed Press
　　Box 7123
　　Berkeley, CA 94707
　　(510) 559-1600

What Color Is Your Parachute?
A Practical Manual for Job-Hunters & Career Changers
　　Richard Nelson Bolles
　　Ten Speed Press
　　Box 7123
　　Berkeley, CA 94707
　　(510) 559-1600

Where Do I Go From Here With My Life?
　　Richard Nelson Bolles and John C. Crystal
　　Ten Speed Press
　　Box 7123
　　Berkeley, CA 94707
　　(510) 559-1600

Other Helpful Books

Amazing Results of Positive Thinking
　　Norman V. Peale
　　Ballantine Books
　　201 E. 50th Street
　　New York, NY 10022
　　(212) 751-2600

Feel the Fear and Do It Anyway
　　Susan Jeffers
　　Fawcett Books
　　201 E. 50th Street
　　New York, NY 10022
　　(800) 733-3000

How to Enjoy Your Life and Your Job: Selections From How to Win Friends and Influence People and *How to Stop Worrying and Start Living*
Dale Carnegie
Pocket Books
1230 Sixth Avenue
New York, NY 10020
(800) 223-2336

Man's Search for Meaning
Viktor Emil Frankl
Pocket Books
1230 Sixth Avenue
New York, NY 10020
(800) 223-2336

On Death and Dying
Elisabeth Kübler-Ross, M.D.
Collier Books
919 Third Avenue
New York, NY 10022
(212) 508-6000

Seven Habits of Highly Effective People
Stephen R. Covey
Simon & Schuster
240 Frisch Court
Paramus, NJ 07652
(201) 751-2600

Swim With the Sharks Without Being Eaten Alive:
Outsell, Outmanage, Outmotivate, and Outnegotiate Your Competition
Harvey Mackay
Ballantine Books
201 E. 50th Street
New York, NY 10022
(212) 751-2600

You Can Negotiate Anything
Herb Cohen
Bantam Books
1540 Broadway
New York, NY 10036
(800) 223-6834

Electronic Resources

Adams JobBank FastRésumé Suite
  Adams Media Corporation
  260 Center Street
  Holbrook, MA 02343
  (617) 767-8100

Career Design
  Career Design Software
  P.O. Box 2086
  Sedona, AZ 86339
  (520) 282-1250

The Emotional IQ Test
  John Mayer, Peter Salovey, and David Caruso
  Virtual Knowledge
  200 Highland Avenue
  Needham, MA 02194
  (800) 301-9545

PFS: Résumé & Job Search Pro for Windows
  Softkey International
  201 Broadway, 6th Floor
  Cambridge, MA 02139-1901
  (800) 323-8088

The Perfect Résumé
  Davidson & Associates
  19840 Pioneer Avenue
  Torrance, CA 90503
  (800) 545-7677

author's note

If you'd like more information about Professionals In Transition Support Group, Inc., please send your request to:

Professionals In Transition
P.O. Box 11252
Winston-Salem, NC 27116-1252

Your feedback and comments about *Career Bounce-Back!* are also welcome. For more information, visit www.jobsearching.org.

—J. Damian Birkel

index

A

acceptance, temporary, 43–44
accomplishments, 63
  quantifying, 97
action plan, for termination, 26–27
anger, 36–39
attitude, winning, 73–74, 108,
  123–125, 133–134
automation, 100

B

bargaining, 39–41
Bolles, Richard Nelson, on job
  hunting, 61, 87
books, 138–143
brevity, 101
bridge burning, 11–27
business card, 134

C

career alternatives, 65–67, 70–71
career books, 138–142
careerbounceback.com, 8, 61, 87
career counseling
  finding right kind of, 84–85
  guarantees for, 85
  low-cost or no-cost alternatives
    for, 85–86
career path diagram, 64
career plan, 9, 69–70, 75
career resources, 10, 137–144
career summary, 72
catastrophizing, 34–36
classified ads, 88, 95, 98–99, 134
coach, 135–136

COBRA, *see* Consolidated Omnibus
  Budget Reconciliation Act
colleagues, 11–27
communication, 54
company resources, use of, 16, 74
compensation, negotiating for,
  14–16, 119–120, 130–131
confidence, projection of, 24, 108,
  123–125
Consolidated Omnibus Budget
  Reconciliation Act, 17–18, 27
cover letter, 81, 92–94, 108, 134
  electronic, 99–102
  guidelines for crafting of, 98–99
  help with, 102–103
  and surviving the cut, 94
  types of, 98
crazies, 53
creditors, 55

D

daily routine, 73
database of job hunters, 100
death and dying, coping with,
  7, 30–31
denial, 31, 33–34
depression, 30–31, 41–43
dreams, launching, 65–67
dress, professional, 124–125

E

electronic job search, 86–90
electronic resources, 144
electronic résumé/cover letter, 99–101
electronic tools, 90

emotional wave (e-wave), 30–45,
   see also grieving process
employer
   meeting needs of, 134
   parting company productively with,
      11–27
executive placement firms, 9, 79
exercise, to combat depression, 43, 53
exit date, timing of, 15
expectations, in job interview, 126
experience
   comparison of, 63
   learning from, 60–61
   looking back at, 62

F

face-saving, 19–20
family
   establishing new role in, 55
   financial issues of, 50–51
   as grounding force, 48–49
   guiding through unemployment
      challenges, 47–58
   maintaining normality of, 55–57
   rising tensions in, 52–53
   steps to maintaining stability of,
      53–58
   threat to role in, 50–51
   weaknesses of, 47–48
family members, assigning money-
   saving tasks to, 52
family wave (f-wave), 49–58
farewell, saying, 22–23
faxing, 99–100
fear, 34–36
feedback
   from interviewers, 121, 127–128
   on résumé, 98
filing system, for networking, 117
finances, 50–52

find e-mail addresses, 89
friends, insights of, 64

G

grieving process, 30–45
   of job loss vs. death, 6–8

H

headhunters, 80, 136
healing process, 8, 49–50
health insurance, 16–18
helplessness, 51–52

I

income, new priorities for, 52
indecisiveness, 35, 120
industry
   doing homework on, 108
   survey of, 67–68
informational interviewing, 109
   ending, 116–117
   filing system for, 117
   following through on, 117
   how to begin, 109–111
   landing, 111–112
   process of, 115–116
   reaching professional for, 113–114
   referrals for, 110
   setting up, 114
   timing tips for, 112–113
insurance benefits, under COBRA,
      16–18
integrity, in networking, 107–108
interview, *see* informational
      interviewing; job interview
interviewing skills, transferable, 121

J

job application, opportunity for, 16
job field, survey of, 67–68
job hunting, *see* job search
job-hunting experience, sharing of, 5–6
job-hunting forums, 86
job-hunting resources, low-cost/ no-cost, 77–90
job-hunting tactics, 10, 133–136
job interview, 9, 119–120
  establishing structure for, 122
  interviewing skills for, 121
  mindset for, 120–121
  projecting winning attitude in, 123–125
  rejection after, 128–129
  second, 127–128
  solving company's problems in, 122–123
  your expectations of, 126
  your needs in, 125–126
job loss
  coping with, 12–13
  emotional symptoms of, 30–32
  grief of, 6–8
  grieving process with, 30–45
  hidden benefits of, 57–58
  inevitability of, 12
  physical and behavioral symptoms of, 30
  truth about, 29–45
job offer, 129–130
  evaluation of, 131
  negotiation of, 130–131
job plan
  putting into action, 73–75
  writing, 69
job savior, 29, 40

job search
  establishing daily routine for, 73
  as full-time job, 55
  headquarters for, 74–75
  high-tech, 86–90
  separating from family life, 56–57
  speeding up, 105–107
  tactics for, 10, 133–136
  tracking results of, 75
  winning attitude in, 73–74
jobsearching.org, 8, 86
job seekers, help for, 1–8
journal keeping, 136

K

keywords, 101
Kübler-Ross, Elisabeth, on grieving process, 7–8, 30

L

labor attorney, 18–19
layoffs, experience of, 3, 12, 14, 33, 110
legal help, during termination process, 18–19

M

magazines, 137–138
mailing envelopes, 135
McClure, Lynne, on managing anger, 38–39
McGee, Chris, 4
McPhail, Pat, career counselor, 5
meeting
  for informational interview, 114–116
  request for, 110–112
mindset
  for informational interview, 108
  for job interview, 120–121
mission statement, personal, 72

mood swings, 29, 44
mortgage payment agreement, 54
moving on, 45
multilevel campaign, 134

N

National Association of Personnel
    Consultants, 82
needs
    of employers, 134
    your, 125–126
negative feelings, 9, 13
negotiation
    of job offer, 130–131
    of severance, 13–16
network
    of allies, 105–118
    rebuilding of, 78
networking, 135
    "backwards," 82
    doing homework for, 108–109
    electronic, 88–90
    to find recruiter, 81–82
    golden rules of, 107–108
    opportunities in, 117–118
    with other job seekers, 86
    to speed up job search, 105–107
    to top, 111
normality, 54–57

O

obituary, writing own, 63–64
office space, creating efficient, 74–75
online directories, 89
online job-hunting services, 86–87
options
    for alternative career, 65–67, 69–71
    considering, 60–61
    evaluation of, 70–71

P

packing, 15, 20–22
panic, 34–36
past experience, 62
pension benefits, 22
pink slips, 1, 14
PIT, *see* Professionals In Transition
PITAs, 6, 8, 10, 133
powerlessness, 51–52
priorities, shift in, 57–58
proaction, 73, 78, 120, 132, 136
problem solver, 122–123
professional network, difficulty of
        penetrating, 5
professional self
    finding, 64–65
    reinvention of, 59–75
Professionals In Transition, 1
    alumni of, 6
    goals of, 5
    meetings of, 1–2, 5–6, 8, 57, 63, 78,
        86, 96, 132–133
    reason for starting, 3–8
    standard agenda for, 5
proprietary information, leaving
        behind, 20–22

Q

quality-of-life issues, 56

R

rapport, 115
reckoning, day of, 12–13
recruitment firms, 79–80
    bias against unemployed of, 80–81
    doing homework on, 82–83
    networking to find, 81–82
    selection of, 79–80
reemployment, shortest path to,
        105–118

Reemployment Toolbox workbook, 61
references
    gathering of, 24–25
    for recruiter, 83
referrals, for informational
        interview, 110
rejection, 9, 44, 49, 75
    dealing with, 127–130
relationships, after termination, 23–24
resources, 137–144
    low-cost/no-cost, 77–90
    online, 86–90
résumé, 9, 61, 72
    electronic, 99–102
    guidelines for crafting of, 96–98
    help with, 102–103
    putting into perspective, 92–93
    and surviving the cut, 94
    value of, 93–94
résumé services, 102–103
*Risky Business: Managing Employee
    Violence in the Workplace*
    (McClure), 38–39
romance, maintaining, 56–57
rumor mill, pre-empting of, 22–23

S

scanning process, 99–101
self-evaluation exercise, 63–64
self marketing, 9
severance
    negotiation of, 13–14
    package, 15–16
severance leverage, 14
shock, 24, 31, 33–34
shouting, 38
skills inventory, 61
software
    for job search, 90, 117
    for résumé writing, 90, 102

spouse
    as partner in reemployment efforts,
        54
    as total fiscal partner, 51–52
stock options, vested, 22
success, campaigning for, 91–103
Switchboard online directory, 89

T

telephone screening process, 112
tension, in family, 52–53
termination
    action plan for, 26–27
    face-saving explanation of, 19–20
    health insurance after, 16–18
    items to take after, 20–22
    legal help during, 18–19
    relationships after, 23–24
thank-you notes, 117, 121, 127
trade shows, 40, 68
training, payment for, 16
transition process, 29–45

U

unemployment
    as great equalizer, 12
    guiding family through challenges
        of, 47–58
    life after, 30–32
    payoffs of, 57–58
    worst effects of, 57–58
unemployment compensation, 25–26

V

vacation pay, with severance, 16
volunteering, 43, 62, 135

W

weaknesses, restated strengths as,
     123–124
What Color Is Your Parachute? (Bolles),
     61
  online services of, 86–87
Wilson, Dr. John P., on grief of job
     loss, 7
winning attitude, 73–74
  projection of, 123–125
  reinforcing, 133–134
work experiences, comparing, 63
World Wide Web (or Web)
  networking on, 89
  tracking hours on, 87–88
worries, prioritization of, 36
worry period, 36
written pitch, 9
written pitches, multiple, 95

CAREER Bounce-Back!
SURFING THE EMOTIONAL WAVE

book, workbook, video

ORDER FORM

Bill to:

_____
name

_____
address 1

_____
address 2

_____
city

_____
state   zip

_____
e-mail (optional)

_____
daytime phone

Ship to:

_____
name

_____
address 1

_____
address 2

_____
city

_____
state   zip

OUR GUARANTEE: Every *Career Bounce-Back!* product is designed to exceed your standards. Our goal is to offer outstanding value for your investment. We will replace your order or refund your money (your choice) for any reason. If you're not satisfied, just return your product and we'll take care of the rest.

❒ VISA ❒ MC ❒ AMEX ❒ DISC ❒ check or money order enclosed

_____   _____
credit card account #   expiration date

_____
signature

	quantity		
Career Bounce-Back! book	_____	@ $14.95 each	$_____.___
Reemployment Toolbox workbook	_____	@ $9.95 each	_____.___
How to Network videotape	_____	@ $29.95 each	_____.___
Complete package (all 3 items)	_____	@ $49.95 each	_____.___

Shipping: per book $3.95 each   _____.___
         per workbook $3.95 each   _____.___
         per videotape $3.95 each   _____.___
         per complete package $4.95 each   _____.___

                          Subtotal   _____.___
NC residents add 6.5% sales tax   _____.___

                          TOTAL $_____.___

CAREER Bounce-Back!
SURFING THE EMOTIONAL WAVE

Mail orders to: Career Bounce-Back!
PO Box 11252, Winston-Salem, NC 27116-1252

CAREER Bounce-Back! SURFING THE EMOTIONAL WAVE

book, workbook, video

ORDER FORM

Bill to:

_____
name

_____
address 1

_____
address 2

_____
city

_____
state   zip

_____
e-mail (optional)

_____
daytime phone

Ship to:

_____
name

_____
address 1

_____
address 2

_____
city

_____
state   zip

OUR GUARANTEE: Every *Career Bounce-Back!* product is designed to exceed your standards. Our goal is to offer outstanding value for your investment. We will replace your order or refund your money (your choice) for any reason. If you're not satisfied, just return your product and we'll take care of the rest.

☐ VISA   ☐ MC   ☐ AMEX   ☐ DISC   ☐ check or money order enclosed

_____   _____
credit card account #   expiration date

_____
signature

	quantity		
Career Bounce-Back! book	_____	@ $14.95 each	$_____.___
Reemployment Toolbox workbook	_____	@ $9.95 each	_____.___
How to Network videotape	_____	@ $29.95 each	_____.___
Complete package (all 3 items)	_____	@ $49.95 each	_____.___

<u>Shipping</u>: per book $3.95 each   _____.___
per workbook $3.95 each   _____.___
per videotape $3.95 each   _____.___
per complete package $4.95 each   _____.___

Subtotal   _____.___
NC residents add 6.5% sales tax   _____.___

TOTAL $_____.___

CAREER Bounce-Back! SURFING THE EMOTIONAL WAVE

<u>*Mail orders to*</u>: Career Bounce-Back!
PO Box 11252, Winston-Salem, NC 27116-1252